Letts
EDUCATIONAL

ADVANCED
SUBSIDIARY

AS
Revision
Notes

Geography

CHECKED   JUL 2008

Author

Peter Goddard

Contents

Shaping the Earth

The atmosphere

Soils and ecosystems

Hydrology

Coasts

Population

Settlement

Industry

Progress check answers

Index

Shaping the Earth

Continental drift and plate tectonics

- The Earth has been in existence for approximately 4 600 million years.
- During that time its character, position and land–sea distribution have changed many times.
- Alfred Wegener devised the theory of continental drift to explain the changes in position of the world's land masses.
- Evidence for continental drift:
  - the similarity of rock structures
  - fossil evidence
  - similar glacial deposits on either side of the Atlantic
  - palaeomagnetic evidence
  - evidence from sea-floor-spreading.
- The Earth's crust comprises eight rigid major plates and a dozen or so smaller ones.

Types of plate boundary

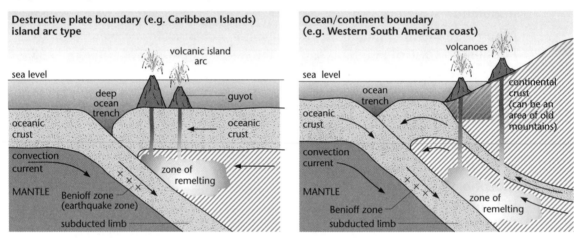

Destructive plate boundary (e.g. Caribbean Islands) island arc type

volcanic island arc

sea level

deep ocean trench

guyot

oceanic crust

oceanic crust

convection current

zone of remelting

MANTLE

Benioff zone (earthquake zone)

subducted limb

Ocean/continent boundary (e.g. Western South American coast)

volcanoes

sea level

ocean trench

continental crust (can be an area of old mountains)

oceanic crust

convection current

MANTLE

Benioff zone

zone of remelting

subducted limb

Consuming or destructive boundaries

- Two types – **subduction zones**, with ocean trenches
        – **island arcs** and **collision zones** with mountain ranges.
- Plates move together and material is destroyed as one plate rides over the top of another.
- Plates are rather like rocky conveyor belts. Material being re-melted deep inside the Earth.
- When continents on separate plates collide, the ground buckles and folds and a new mountain chain is born.
- Most volcanoes and destructive earthquakes are associated with consuming boundaries.

Accreting or constructive boundaries

- The plates move apart, molten material seeps to the surface from the mantle, cools to form new lithosphere.
- Almost all these boundaries lie deep beneath the oceans where they form mid-ocean ridges.
- There is a continuous system of accreting boundary twisting and turning for 47 000 miles around the world.
- Rock that cools at these boundaries becomes magnetised in the direction of the north magnetic pole and then retains this record throughout time. (Used as evidence for continental drift.)

Conservative or transform boundaries

- No material is added or destroyed.
- Two plates grind and slip past each other in a series of jerks, e.g. San Andreas Fault.
- Transform faults occur widely in the fracture zones associated with spreading ridges.
- Caused by pressure, rotation and contraction.

Most of the world's great mountain ranges, its destructive earthquakes and volcanoes occur at the plate boundaries.

The mechanism

- The mechanism that moves the plates is associated with convection currents. Plumes of hot material from the mantle rise and spread under the plates, in so doing they move the plates forward.
- Rafts of lighter granitic continental rocks (SIAL = silica and aluminium) float on denser basaltic oceanic rocks (SIMA = silica and magnesium).
- The principle of flotation or buoyancy is called isostacy. This means that continental plates stand high above the oceanic plates.
- Scientists only became aware of plate structure when good maps of the ocean floor were produced showing underwater mountains, ridges, island arcs, trenches and plains.
- Plate tectonics proved to be a unifying theory – widely accepted by the late 1960s.
- Many theories are comparatively recent!

The pattern of change

- The continents were once joined to form one landmass: Pangaea (all lands) made up of Gondwanaland (to the south) and Laurasia (to the north).
- It began splitting about 200 million years ago.
- It is probable that a single continent existed 700 million years ago before breaking up.
- By 570 million years ago four continents were moving about the globe.
- It is predicted that a new super-continent will form again 200 million years from now with the centre of the old Pangaea becoming the coastlines of the new landmass.

Examiner's Tip

The processes and evidence of plate movement is a popular theme to draw AS Level questions from.

Volcanoes

- These play a key role in shaping the planet.
- They probably created our atmosphere and definitely released water vapour onto the surface of the planet, creating the oceans.
- Every year about 50 of the Earth's 700 active volcanoes erupt.

Anatomy of a volcano

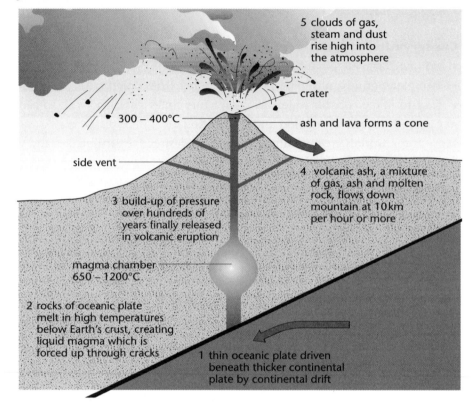

5 clouds of gas, steam and dust rise high into the atmosphere

crater

ash and lava forms a cone

300 – 400°C

side vent

4 volcanic ash, a mixture of gas, ash and molten rock, flows down mountain at 10km per hour or more

3 build-up of pressure over hundreds of years finally released in volcanic eruption

magma chamber 650 – 1200°C

2 rocks of oceanic plate melt in high temperatures below Earth's crust, creating liquid magma which is forced up through cracks

1 thin oceanic plate driven beneath thicker continental plate by continental drift

- Volcanoes are typically conical in shape, though this depends on the nature of the material and type of eruption.
- They are classified in a number of ways, i.e. type of flow, type of eruption and level of activity.

Volcanic hazards

- *Lava flows* Two main types are **aa** and **pahoehoe**. When hot enough lava flows like water, e.g. Mount Etna on Sicily.
- *Lahars* These are torrents of mud, moving at 90 km/h, e.g. Armero, at the head of the Langunilla Valley in Colombia.
- *Pyroclastic/tephra clouds* Solid material such as dust, ash, and cinders that is thrown from the volcano, e.g. Mount Pinatubo, Philippines.
- *Gases* From CO_2 to hydrogen sulphide, e.g. Lake Nyos in Cameroon, West Africa.
- *Nueé Ardenteé* A mixture of superheated rock and gas, e.g. Mount St Helens.
- *Jokulhlaups* Outbursts of water caused by a build up of sub-glacial meltwater due to volcanic activity, e.g. Loki under the Vatnajokull ice-sheet in Iceland.
- *Tsunamis* Form when water is vertically displaced, e.g. Krakatoa in 1883.
- *Other dangers* include landslides, fire, disease, and volcanic winters (where atmospheric ash blocks out the sun, and crop yields drop).

Examiner's Tip

Don't forget that volcanoes also occur at hotspots.

Volcanic predictability

- Scientists are becoming increasingly proficient at predicting volcanic eruptions.
- The main methods of prediction focus on assessing the pre-cursors to eruption.
  - *Seismometers* measure earthquake activity which increases near a volcanic eruption.
  - *Gas levels* sulphur emissions increase near an eruption.
  - *Lasers/tiltmeters* detect changes in the slope of the volcano and assess swelling of the cone.
  - *Ultra sound* is increasingly utilised to monitor changes.
  - *Thermal* anomalies are also measured to assess activity.

Responding to the volcano hazard

- Little can be done to control volcanoes.
- Only lava has been successfully dealt with, e.g. Eldafells lavaflow on Heimaey, Iceland was halted in 1973 with water sprays and Etna's lava by damming and banking in 1983.
- Barriers and conduits have been built in Indonesia to guide lava and lahars away from vulnerable areas.
- Steep and strengthened ash-shedding roofs have been built in the Philippines.
- In other areas like Montserrat people physically move their house!
- At best a 'volcanic' community can be prepared for disaster. Through accurate land-use planning, hazard assessment and mapping and through utilising overseas technical know-how and aid resources before, during and after events many of the effects can be negated.

Why do people continue to live in volcanically active areas?

- **Lava weathers to give fertile soils**, e.g. Indonesia, the West Indies.
- **Precious stones and minerals** form in such areas, e.g. South Africa.
- Superheated water can be used for **geothermal power**, e.g. Iceland.
- Areas are **tourist attractors**, e.g. Tenerife and Lanzarote.
- Products of vulcanicity can be **used for building**, e.g. ignimbrite blocks.

Earthquakes

- Over the globe there are probably 500 000 earthquakes/year of which a hundred or so will do damage. They account for about 10% of natural disaster deaths per year.
- Earthquakes are basically shock waves that are transmitted from a focus, which can lie anywhere from the surface to 700 km beneath the Earth's crust.
- The most damaging quakes have foci that are close to the surface and tend to arise along active plate boundaries.
- Earthquakes result from sudden movements along geological faults, bumping and grinding against each other in response to convection currents in the deep mantle rocks of the crust (or because of volcanic eruptions).
- Earthquakes generate a variety of shock waves. Three types of seismic wave have been identified, P (primary or push) waves, S (secondary or shear) waves and L (surface or long) waves. The speed of these waves varies according to the properties of the rocks through which they pass (P waves are the fastest and surface waves the slowest). P waves are compressional in nature, they tend not to be as damaging as the shear and surface waves. Shear waves cause the first shaking motion, vibration occurring at right angles to the direction of travel.
- Surface waves have the potential to shake large areas of the globe.
- The energy required to set the ground in motion cannot be maintained. The effect is rapidly over, and damage tends to be confined to small areas.

Examiner's Tip

Remember volcanoes and earthquakes are environmental hazards; that is they have the potential to harm humans and their possessions.

(Continued next page)

Earthquakes

Magnitude and intensity

- This depends on:
  - the depth of shock origin
  - the nature of the surface layer, e.g. soft material amplifies the shock
  - the nature of the overlying material, e.g. hard rock absorbs/soft amplifies.

Effects

- Vertical or lateral displacements of the crust.
- Raising and lowering of the sea floor.
- Landslides, liquefaction and tsunami.

Measurement

- Earthquake magnitude is measured on the Richter Scale, using a seismometer.
- Each unit on the Richter Scale represents a ×10 increase in wave amplitude.
- Intensity is measured on the Mercalli Scale.

Impact

- This is often greater in LEDCs than it is in MEDCs.
- In LEDCs building regulations are poor, they are remote and isolated, emergency planning is non-existent.

Two examples are offered below:

Maharashtra/Khilari September 1993 – LEDC	Loma Prieta, San Francisco and San Jose October 1989 – MEDC
25 000 killed. A shallow focus, 6.4 on the Richter Scale, in an area where there had been no tremors for years. 50 villages and towns affected. 7000 homes destroyed. The high deaths toll relates to the timing of the quake, it happened during the night! *Problems:* Dealing with the injured. 90 villages/ 200 000 people needed new homes. Delay in dealing with the problem. Lack of long-term transfer technologies	62 killed. 7.1 on the Richter Scale. 12 000 displaced. $6 billion of damage. Deaths, injuries and socio-economic disruption were limited because of the state of California's preparedness. *Problems:* Marina District wrecked by liquefaction, Cypress Freeway destroyed and Pacific Garden Mall damaged. All the damage was restored within a few months.

Responding to the earthquake hazard

Factors determining whether earthquake management is successful

Physical factors
- time of day
- depth of focus
- base geology
- duration of the shake
- location of the epicentre

Human factors
- building style
- preparedness
- efficiency of the emergency services
- ability to cope and react

Other factors
- pinpointing of weaknesses in the infrastructure
- identification of localities prone to liquefaction/folding or faulting
- charting of the recurrence interval

Possible actions

- Modify (change) the event, e.g. hazard-resistant design.
- Modify a community's vulnerability to reduce losses, e.g. prediction and warning (though neither are reliable).
- Modify the effects of loss to the community through aid and insurance.

Natural hazards

- There is a clear link between national income levels and deaths.
- Numbers of deaths also relate to the size of the hazard, the levels of adjustment to it, population density and perception of the hazard threat.

Rocks and relief

Igneous rocks

- **Granite** is a coarse-grained intrusive igneous rock consisting of three minerals: quartz (resistant), feldspar (susceptible to chemical weathering) and mica.
- The largest form of granite structure are batholiths, but granite can occur in other forms such as dykes (vertical) and sills (horizontal).

Linton's theory of tor formation

- About 450 million years ago, cooling magma formed granite batholiths 6000 metres below the present-day surface of Dartmoor.
- Percolating groundwater caused chemical weathering by hydration and hydrolysis especially in zones which are jointed.
- Subsequent removal of the overlying sedimentary strata exposed the unweathered remnants of the batholith as tors, for example Hound Tor.
- The horizontal divisions between the blocks are pseudo-bedding planes; the result of pressure release as the overburden is reduced by denudation.

Sedimentary rocks

Carboniferous limestone

- Found at Malham in North Yorkshire, is composed of calcium carbonate. It displays horizontal bedding and vertical jointing and thus possesses secondary permeability.
- The best known feature of karst landscapes is the limestone pavement, comprising clints (blocks) and grykes (vertical joints).
- The chemical weathering process of carbonation enlarges the grykes.
- Other karstic landforms include sinkholes, caves and resurgent streams.

Dry valleys

- These are also typical in limestone and chalk.
- During periglacial periods of the Pleistocene, when underlying rock was frozen solid, surface run-off eroded the dry valleys.

Chalk

- This is a form of limestone, but with different amounts of calcite and dolomite.

Comparison of typical chalk and limestone scenery:

	South Downs (chalk)	Yorkshire Dales (limestone)
Descriptors	Billowy, rounded and smooth soft profiles.	Broken, scarred and chiselled, a strong angular look.
Structure	Gulled, and frequent coombes. The questa with its escarpments and dip slope.	Terraced into beds, pavements, sinkholes and caves.
Water	Chalk is permeable and lacks perennial streams. Flow of rivers is affected by the position of the water table. Many winter-borne streams exist, Streams tend to be widely spaced. Resurgences are rare.	The solubility of limestone means it lacks the dendritic development of the river systems found on chalk. Limestone tends to exhibit few rivers: it is a 'dry' landscape. Resurgences are common.
Slope foot	Sludge and coombe deposits.	Angular shattered debris.

Metamorphic rocks

- Formed from either igneous or sedimentary rocks by renewed heat and/or pressure.
- Examples include: marble from limestone and slate from shale.
- All metamorphic rocks are impervious (they will not allow the infiltration of water).

Examiner's Tip

A number of AS Level specifications do request certain rocks and rock groups for study. Does your specification require such knowledge?

Weathering

- The disintegration and decomposition of rocks, *in situ* (in one place), by natural agents at or near the Earth's surface.
- It is different from erosion, which requires moving agents.
- Denudation is the general term given to the wearing away of the Earth's surface by weathering and erosion.
- There are three main types of weathering.

Physical weathering:

Frost shattering or freeze-thaw

- This relies on water in crack subjected to many freeze-thaw cycles.
- Water expands by 9.6% of its volume as it freezes; exerting a stress of up to 2100 kg/cm^2 at $-22°C$.

Salt crystallisation

- Caused by the crystallisation of solutions of salts occupying fissures and pore spaces within rocks, e.g. sodium chloride.
- As the crystals grow pressure causes surface scaling or granular disintegration.

Insolation weathering or exfoliation

- Occurs in desert environments with a large diurnal range in temperature.
- Rock is a poor conductor of heat, so inner layers of rock remain cold despite changes of surface temperature.
- Outer layers are subject to alternate expansion (due to intense daytime heating) and contraction (due to rapid cooling at night).
- The outer layers eventually peel off.

Pressure release or dilatation

- Occurs in many rocks; especially those that have developed at considerable pressure and depth.
- If these rocks are exposed at a later date to the atmosphere (due to removal of the overburden by, for example, glacial erosion) then there will be a substantial release of pressure (at right angles).
- This weakens the rock allowing other agents to enter it and other processes to occur.

Chemical weathering

- This contributes to the disintegration of rocks in a number of ways.
- It weakens the coherence between minerals.
- It attacks the cements, e.g. in sandstone.
- It forms solutions, which are washed out by rain, making the rock porous and so ready to crumble by granular disintegration.
- It causes the formation of alteration products.
- There are four main processes, hydration, hydrolysis, oxidation and carbonation.

Hydration

- Occurs in all rocks.
- Certain crystals grow in size due to the addition of water.
- This creates stresses in the rock, which may eventually crumble and disintegrate (granular disintegration).

Hydrolysis

- Occurs in rocks containing the mineral feldspar (e.g. granite).
- Hydrolysis is a chemical reaction between water and the hydrogen ions in the rock.

Oxidation

- Occurs in rocks containing iron compounds.
- Oxygen dissolved in water reacts with the iron to form oxides and hydroxides.

Carbonation

- Occurs in rocks contain calcium carbonate.
- Carbon dioxide in the atmosphere is absorbed by rain, creating a weak carbonic acid.
- Rocks are dissolved and carried away in solution.

Biological weathering

- Plant roots widen cracks in rock faces; rotting plants create humic acid (a chelate) and animals produce uric acid, which chemically decomposes the rock.

Examiner's Tip

Remember other variables influence weathering, e.g. microclimate, altitude, slope angle aspect, geology and people.

Slopes

- Slopes form much of the Earth's surface and influence most aspects of geography including land use, farming, transport networks, rivers and their basins.
- Many slopes are unstable and changing all of the time, sometimes rapidly, while the shallowest slopes 'creep'.
- Slope shapes are mostly due to past slope movement.
- Weathering processes produce debris, which is transported downslope by processes of mass movement.

Mass movement processes

- These may be sub-divided into rapid and slow, wet and dry.
- The type of process involved and its velocity depend on many factors including the angle of slope, the amount of water present in the waste material, the degree and type of vegetation, and human activity.
- Slope movements on soft rocks occur rapidly, and differ from the movements that occur on hard rock.
- The most common mass movements are those that occur through gravity on soft rocks.
- Most of these movements are rapid and occur over a clearly defined boundary, called a slip surface or shear plane.
- The loose debris at the foot of a slope is termed *talus*.
- The form (profile/angle) of a slope depends on the balance between subaerial supply of talus by weathering and mass movement processes and its removal at the cliff foot by, for example, a river or the sea.

Types of movement

- *Soil creep* This is very slow, does not require a lot of water and is the result of surface material being 'heaved' down slope.
- *Solifluction* Occurs in periglacial climates. The ground tends to be wet (in the summer) and movements are relatively fast.
- *Cliff collapse* This rapid slope movement occurs on steep slopes.
- *Mudflows* When very wet this occurs very rapidly.

Translational slides   **Rotational slides**   **Multiple rotational slides**

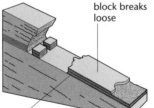
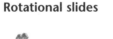
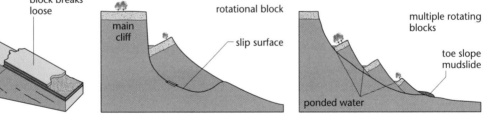

Translational slides The slip surface is parallel to the slope and they are not very deep. Heavy rainfall over a period of time can start them off.

Rotational slides Large blocks of material rotate over a curved slip surface. The ground surface is left tilting back towards the main cliff. Often a number of blocks rotate down the hill giving a step-like slope profile.

Mudslides These usually occur in debris that has already slipped downslope. High water content means that they can flow at fast speeds for long periods.

Examiner's Tip

Diagrams are a good medium through which to learn the terminology and processes to do with slopes.

Progress check

1 State the evidence for plate tectonics using the following headings:

   (a) Jigsaw fit of the continents

   (b) Distribution of earthquakes

   (c) Palaeomagnetism

2 Aireys hypothesis: 'wooden blocks floating in water are thought to mirror continental crust and to explain variations in thickness'.

   (a) What happens when ice forms over mountain areas?

   (b) What happens when the processes of denudation get to work over mountains?

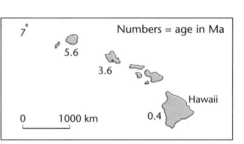

3 (a) Copy and label the destructive plate boundary on page 4.

   (b) On your diagram add the position of possible volcanoes.

   (c) Why does one plate descend below the other?

4 Draw a cross-section to illustrate how a plate moving across a hot spot has produced the situation shown, right.

7°	Numbers = age in Ma
5.6	
	3.6
	Hawaii
0 1000 km	0.4

5 'Volcanoes do more good than harm.' Produce a list of the positive contributions that volcanoes make to man.

6

Wave type	Speed	Passes through?	Motion
P waves	Slow / fast	Liquid / solid	Compressional / displacement Right-angled / rolling
S waves	Slow / fast	Liquid / solid	Compressional / displacement Right-angled / rolling
L waves	Slow / fast	Liquid / solid	Compressional / displacement Right-angled / rolling

Quiet

Record

Copy out the table:

   (a) Delete to leave the word or words that correctly identify the speed, ability of waves to pass through the earth and the motion of earthquakes.

   (b) Add the words L wave, P wave or S wave to the above seismic trace.

7 For one of your earthquake case studies outline:

   (a) When did the earthquake occur? What were its causes and characteristics?

   (b) What were the consequences of the earthquake and what lessons were learned?

8 Mass movement is the rapid movement of weathered rock downslope. Two types of movement are slides and flows. Draw annotated diagrams to show how they differ.

Answers on page 89

The atmosphere

Atmospheric processes

- The study of the atmosphere is demanding because of the complexity of the processes and mechanism that power, run and maintain it.
- The atmosphere is an open system – with flows or movements of energy and materials between the different parts of the system. The sun is the driving force.

Energy in the atmosphere

- *Solar radiation, or insolation*, occurs as short-wave radiation and is the main source of external (heat) energy input into the Earth's atmosphere system.
- The atmosphere is reasonably 'transparent' to solar radiation, in that large amounts of energy are allowed to pass through to the ground surface.
- This stream of energy powers the atmosphere and the biosphere.
- About 50% of the insolation received at the edge of the atmosphere is actually absorbed.
- Most insolation is scattered (by dust), reflected (by clouds) or absorbed (by clouds, dust and water vapour).
- *Long-wave radiation* emitted by terrestrial and atmospheric radiation is largely absorbed; this contrasts with solar radiation.
- *The balance of the energy receipts* is used to heat the ground and air, by conduction, convection, turbulence and evaporation.
- Energy varies across the Earth's surface: global variations relate to latitude, and temporal variations to seasonal shifts in radiation, and land and sea distribution.
- The Earth's motions and gravitational pull (on air masses and moisture) provide a constant internal source of energy.

The atmosphere on the move

- Uneven heating of the Earth's surface causes variations in air pressure; producing air movement or wind.
- Movement in the atmosphere is probably the most obvious of its characteristics.
- The study of the forces that control movement is fundamental to understanding how energy (as heat) is distributed around the globe by the global circulation.
- *Advection is* horizontal air movement.
- *Convection is* vertical movement.
- *Pressure gradient* (air density variations) between places, causes air to move between high and low pressure locations.
- *The convection cell model* builds on work by George Hadley (in 1735) and William Ferrel (in 1889) (see diagram).

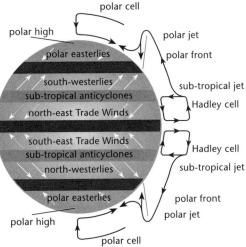

polar cell
polar high
polar jet
polar front
polar easterlies
south-westerlies
sub-tropical jet
sub-tropical anticyclones
Hadley cell
north-east Trade Winds
south-east Trade Winds
sub-tropical anticyclones
Hadley cell
north-westerlies
sub-tropical jet
polar easterlies
polar front
polar high
polar jet
polar cell

- ⬛ *low pressure areas*
- ⬜ *high pressure areas*
- → *Jet stream*

(Continued next page)

Atmospheric processes

- Air circulates in a conventional fashion, but there are consequences for the atmosphere related to this movement.
- *The equation of state* involves the rate at which the air can rise or fall.
- *The thermodynamic equation* determines the ability of air to expand or contract.
- *The equation of continuity* reveals how air will continually circulate.
- *The Coriolis Effect* is the apparent deflection of moving objects due to the Earth's perceived rotation.
- In the mid-latitudes the pressure gradient and Coriolis force are in balance.
- Geostrophic wind, air flowing parallel to the isobars, between areas of high and low pressure, results from this balance.

Global air movements

- These occur at a variety of scales.
- There is a close relationship between major winds and the world's pressure systems.
- Windbelts also contain the world's major weather systems.

Mid-latitude movements

- *Complex upper air movements* are found between the polar and tropical circulations.
- *The circumpolar vortex*, powerful Ferrel Westerlies combine with the jet streams in the mid-latitudes to affect surface weather/winds and pressure systems.
- *Rossby Waves* are the series of waves that build up surface winds and weather belts.
- Rossby waves form because of the Earth's thermal differences, the rotation of the Earth, and because of the destabilising effect of mountain ranges.
- *The index cycle* is the link between the Rossby waves, jet streams and weather systems in the low and high-pressure circulation.
- *Jet streams* are fast (200 km/hr) and found at about 12 000 m.
- They appear where warm and cold air mix.
- They guide weather systems (W to E) in the Northern Hemisphere.
- Shifts in their location can affect our weather for long periods.

Influence of atmospheric movement

- It provides water for the hydrological cycle.
- It absorbs and redistributes energy, e.g. the Gulf Stream and North Atlantic Drift benefits Western Europe by releasing heat to warm and provide a milder climate than might otherwise be the case.
- Warmed oceans and their currents can therefore affect local and distant locations, e.g. El Niño and La Niña.

Examiner's Tip

The effect of El Niño is significant. The mechanism of this phenomenon needs to be understood.

Moisture in the atmosphere

- *Water* is probably the most important mass moved by the air/atmosphere, with temperature defining the condition or state of the energy held.
- *Air* is mostly in its highest energy state as vapour but in the UK liquid (rain) and frozen forms (snow and ice) are common.
- The amount of moisture in the atmosphere is relatively small, but highly varied in time and space.
- *Saturated air* is air holding the maximum amount of water vapour possible. (Remember warm air holds more moisture than cold air.)
- *The water-vapour content* of the air can be expressed in terms of its absolute humidity or, more commonly, in terms of its relative humidity.
- *Relative humidity* is the percentage ratio between the actual amount of water and the maximum amount that the air can hold at that temperature.

Two methods of precipitation formation exist

1 *Bergeron – Findeison Theory* says that water droplets are lifted rapidly by turbulent air currents.
   - Rapid freezing occurs and water vapour turns instantly to ice through sublimation.
   - As ice falls from the clouds it melts and turns to rain.

2 *Coalescence Theory* says that water droplets grow in turbulent air.
   - Large clouds form and droplets grow and eventually fall.
   - Collision in the clouds cause the drops to grow.

- *Types of precipitation* include: rain, drizzle, hail, snow, sleet, fog, fog drip, dew.

Condensation

- *Clouds* are condensation mostly at high levels.
- Fogs, condensation at or near the ground.
- They occur when air is brought to saturation point or its dew-point temperature.
- Condensation is assisted in the atmosphere by condensation nuclei around which liquid water can form.
- Condensation only leads to precipitation when gravity overcomes the ability of air currents to keep the water vapour buoyant.
- *Air cooling*, principally by the vertical ascent of air, causes most saturation and condensation in the atmosphere to take place.
- Air is forced to rise and cool by:
  - orographic uplift
  - frontal uplift
  - large-scale convergence and ascent in low-pressure systems
  - smaller-scale convective currents.

Examiner's Tip

Remember: cooling → condensation and cloud.

When: air contacts cold ground or oceans, when it cools adiabatically or when warm air mixes with colder air.

Lapse rates

Stability of the air

- *Advectional processes* continually seek to establish a stable atmosphere, in terms of the distribution of energy.
- *Air masses* with their uniform temperature and humidity typify this stability.
- *Adiabatic (vertical) movement* within air masses of small parcels/pockets/balloons or bubbles of air as air masses moving over irregular relief or variably heated land masses has dramatic effects, in terms of local weather.

The influence of lapse rates

- *The ELR (Environmental Lapse Rate)* describes how in general, temperature falls as you move higher into the atmosphere.
- *The DALR (Dry Adiabatic Lapse Rate)* is the fixed rate at which non-saturated air cools. Cooling happens when pockets of rising air gain height, expand, lose further (kinetic) energy and cool still further.
- *The SALR (Saturated Adiabatic Lapse Rate)* is half the rate of the DALR. Once rising air reaches the condensation level it becomes saturated. Latent heat is produced and water vapour turns to water reducing air cooling.
- *Internal pressure change* not heat exchange, causes the adiabatic changes outlined above. They occur in a vertical direction.
- *Temperature varies with height*
  - ELR = 6.5°C/km climbed
  - DALR = 10°C/km climbed
  - SALR = 6°C/km climbed

  N.B. These rates vary at the same rate up or down!

Air stability

- This is an important concept.
- Its character is determined by the relationship between the ELR and both the DALR and SALR, which influence temperature.
- It determines the buoyancy of the air and thus the development of cloud and fog.
- *Unstable* air occurs when the ELR is greater than the DALR and SALR.
- If initially uplifted, a vertically displaced air parcel is encouraged to rise still further.
- If initially forced downward an air parcel will continue to descend.
- *Stable air* A parcel of air displaced vertically upwards or downwards in the atmosphere will tend to return to its original position. Here the ELR is less than the DALR or SALR. Cumulus clouds, often of large vertical extent, are characteristic of unstable air. Horizontally developed stratus clouds tend to form in more stable air.

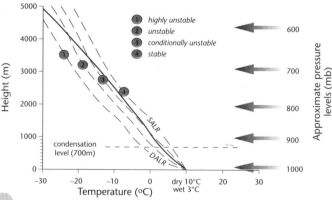

Many students find lapse rates the single most puzzling aspect of the whole Geography course. To understand weather you have to understand lapse rates.

Britain and Western Europe's weather and climate

Britain has a Cool Temperate Humid (Maritime) Climate.

- This is typically found in the mid-latitudes between 40° and 60° N (or S).
- Marine influences predominate, and can influence areas far inland.
- Eastward moving air brings depressions (cyclonic conditions) with characteristics of temperature and humidity derived from the oceans.
- The weather can be extremely changeable and variable (e.g. continental high pressure extends at times causing severe cold and within hours southwesterly flow is re-established and warm damp conditions reappear).
- Winters are mild, the oceans affect is marked.
- Summers are warm, 13° to 18°C is common in July.
- The oceans can cool summer temperatures too.
- Drought conditions are rare; but the ingress of North African air can bring spells of prolonged hot weather.
- Rain occurs throughout the year; but does vary from place to place based on the relief. (It chiefly runs in on cyclonic fronts and decreases to the East.)
- Depressions (cyclonic conditions, lows) are less common in summer than in winter and generally bring warm but wet conditions.
- Anticyclones bring hot, sunny weather in summer and fog, snow, cold and still conditions in winter.

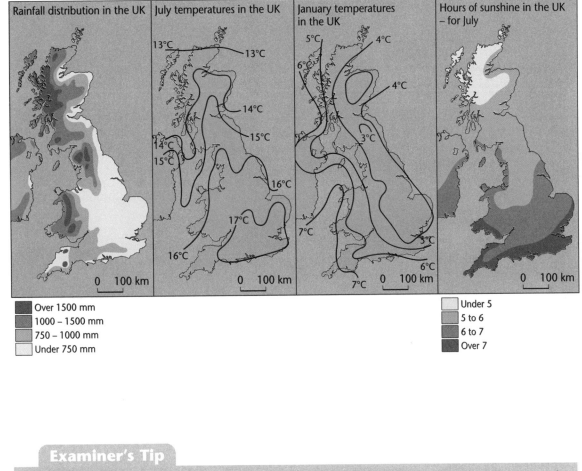

Rainfall distribution in the UK

Over 1500 mm
1000 – 1500 mm
750 – 1000 mm
Under 750 mm

July temperatures in the UK

January temperatures in the UK

Hours of sunshine in the UK – for July

Under 5
5 to 6
6 to 7
Over 7

High and low pressure

Low pressure

What is it?

- If an area has pressure that is lower than its surroundings, then it is termed low pressure.
- Cyclones and depressions are low-pressure systems.

High pressure

What is it?

- If an area has pressure that is greater than its surroundings, then it is termed a high-pressure area.
- Anticyclones are high-pressure systems.

Average world atmospheric pressure = 1013 Mb

What are the weather effects?

- Unstable rising air cause unsettled and changeable weather.
- Typically depressions bring:
  - cloudy skies
  - low levels of sunshine
  - wet weather
  - temperatures that are mild for the time of year
  - windy conditions
  - changeable weather.

What are the weather effects?

- Typically these pressure belts bring stable weather conditions:
  - clear skies
  - sunshine
  - dry weather
  - high day and low night temperatures
  - calm weather
  - dew and frost
  - fog and mist
  - thunderstorms
  - snow in winter.

Air masses

- Air above the Earth's surfaces which develops characteristics which replicate those over which they have passed.
- Air masses have many origins causing weather to be very variable.

Severe weather and related phenomena

- Extremes of precipitation and temperature cause most of our weather hazards.
- Extremes of air movement surprisingly create a more minor effect.

Tropical cyclones

- These are classified differently around the world.
- *Cyclones* hit Southern Asia (between June and November).
- *The Willy Willies* hit Australia (between January and March).
- *Typhoons* hit the Western Pacific (between July and October). Typically these generate winds of between 40 and 119 km/hr.
- *Hurricanes* are common on the Gulf coast of the eastern seaboard of the USA between August and October. Winds in the order of 119 to 300 km/hr are common.

Hurricanes

- Associated with specific atmospheric and ocean conditions.
- Intense low-pressure systems (commonly less than 920 mb) form between 30°N and 30°S, the *Intertropical Convergence Zone*.
- As the *Coriolis Effect* is at its greatest near the equator, the hurricane systems rotation is easily initiated.
- In summer sea temperatures exceed the minimum 26° to 27°C necessary for latent heat to be released (because of condensation of water vapour) to strengthen the hurricane (relative humidity of 60% is common).
- Towering (15 km is common) cumulo-nimbus clouds form around the central eye in highly unstable conditions.
- These clouds further fuel the hurricane as latent heat energy exchanges moisture from gas to liquid.

Examiner's Tip

Hurricanes are frequent in the late summer months. Keep a log of up-to-date examples, from the newspapers.

- Spinning weather sub-systems develop all around the main hurricane mass.
- The ocean then provides the initiating and sustaining energy for hurricanes. They quickly 'die' once they move onto the land.
- The high levels of moisture held also point to a sea origin (typically in the order of 10 to 25 cm/day).
- *The effects of hurricanes include:*
  - storm surges
  - damage to property
  - agricultural damage
  - huge insurance claims
  - effect on tourism

Tornadoes

- These are a concentration of cyclonically spinning air, a super cell (about 100 miles across), found overland, rather than over water.
- Most often a visible cloud forms from a large cumulonimbus origin.
- The tremendous rotations are initiated by rapid convergence at the base of the cumulonimbus cloud, as rapid updraughts develop.
- Tornadoes are common over the mid-west and southern states of the USA during the heat of early summer afternoons.
- The funnel is visible because of pressure drops, cooling and consequent saturation.
- Tornadoes are measured on the Fujita F1 to 5 scale.

The SE Asian Monsoon

- Is the major disturber of the global atmospheric circulation.
- It displaces masses of energy to the North and South between 60° and 180°E.

Causes

- *Differentials in heat absorption and cooling of land and sea* creates pressure changes and winds.
- *Inter tropical discontinuity* and its wind belts shift seasonally.
- *Mountains* influence the patterns of rainfall.
- *Reduced CO_2 concentrations* due to uplift over the Himalayas causes less heat to be absorbed, which leads to cooling.
- *Jet streams* change position creating two markedly different monsoon periods.

The winter monsoon

- Westerly jets split around the Tibetan Plateau.
- Descending air causes high pressure over central Asia.
- This causes out-blowing northeast winds across Asia, causing clear skies, little rain and sunny weather.

The summer monsoon

- In March–June, the northern jet dominates the area.
- The overhead sun migrates over India.
- The ITD moves to an area south of the Himalayas.
- Low pressure moves northwards, the so-called monsoon trough. Low pressure continues to deepen and develop over the area, pulling in warm moist air from the North Indian Ocean and causing intense rainfall.

Impacts

- Agricultural yields increase during the 'good' monsoon years.
- Flooding and loss of life are also common.

Examiner's Tip

A number of the AS specifications require a knowledge of the monsoon climate.

How weather affects the economy

Agriculture

- *Animals and livestock*, particularly young ones, are distressed by excessive heat or cold.
- *Fodder and grazing* for animals can be difficult to provide in winter.
- *Crops* are affected by day-to-day weather fluctuations. Few grow above 60°N or S.
- A late frost affects the coffee crop. Droughts are threat to crops.
- Pests tend to be weather dependent (e.g. locusts).

Construction

- Concrete laying and groundwork does not happen in extreme cold or wet periods.
- Tenders are often adjusted to allow for weather risks.

Fishing

- Is completely weather dependent.
- Icing of the superstructure leads to disasters, as do storm conditions.

Transport

- Bad/adverse weather causes delays and accidents.
- Local highway divisions can save by only gritting where necessary.
- Shipping saves fuel and time all by using forecasting to improve efficiency.

Power

- There is a strong and obvious link between weather and fuel used.
- Utilities use past weather records to anticipate times of great demand.

Television

- Reception is affected by rapid changes in temperature and humidity.
- Anticyclonic conditions in particular affect reception.

Business and retail

- In summer supermarkets stock up on BBQ fuels and foods, salad products and fruit.
- In winter, stocks of antifreeze and batteries for cars sell quickly and pharmacists dispense more medicine.
- In wet weather, plumbers attend more leaks and bursts. Tourists spend more money in retail outlets.

Leisure and sport

- Adverse weather has a dramatic effect on sport of all kinds.

Health, housing, dress and way of life

- Cultural traditions relate to the weather and climate of peoples' home areas.

Global concerns

Damage to the ozone layer

- Ozone is a thin layer found in the stratosphere, 10 km to 50 km above the ground.
- Being very unstable, ozone is easily broken down by high-energy UV light; the process of breakdown causes absorption.
- This blocking effect is beneficial to us because high-intensity UV can cause skin cancer.
- Ozone is being depleted by mans' use of CFCs (Chlorofluorocarbons) in industry, as a coolant in refrigerators and in aerosol propellants.
- Once released CFCs rise high in the atmosphere, releasing chlorine, which destroys ozone.

- Chlorine is released readily in the cold (below –80°C) sunless skies of the Poles.

Smog

- The smog we experience today is vastly different from that of the 1950s.
- Today we have to deal with more lethal photochemical smog produced by the exhaust gases of vehicles and industry.
- Still, warm, clear sunny conditions allow the build up of poisonous ground-level ozone.
- Small amounts at ground level can be lethal, affecting breathing, causing conjunctivitis-type irritations, and affecting plant and animal tissue.

Examiner's Tip

The threats to our atmosphere are topical and frequently appear in AS Level exams.

The greenhouse effect and global warming

- Warming near the Earth's surface results in the atmosphere trapping the Sun's heat: without the greenhouse effect the Earth would be 33°C cooler.
- CO_2 is a major contributor to the greenhouse effect and with water vapour it reflects vast amounts of heat.
- Once emitted a CO_2 molecule stays active in the atmosphere for about 200 years.
- It should be remembered that global warming has been widely debated, that climate varies naturally and that data supporting the theory is difficult to verify.

Acid rain

- Quantities of sulphur dioxide and oxides of nitrogen are emitted into the atmosphere from industrial activity and vehicles.
- In the atmosphere chemical changes turn rain into weak acids (in the order of pH 4.3).

Aspects of local climate

Air flow in mountains (anabatic and katabatic winds)

- During the day when conditions are calm, warm air blows up the valley, in response to the heating of the air in contact with the valley slopes.
- A return wind at night completes the circulation as the reverse happens.
- Accumulations of cold air in valley bottoms can cause frost hollows to form.

Land and sea breezes

- On warm days air over the land heats up and expands, tilting the pressure gradient.
- The result is a small circulatory system, air moves towards the land at low level, with a compensating outblowing wind aloft.
- The reverse happens at night.
- These breezes have a marked effect on coastal climates.

Mountain climates

- Few mountain climates fit into any climate scheme easily.
- For instance in tropical areas increases in height are the equivalent of an increase in latitude.
- In Africa and other equatorial continents and countries mountains are important for their effect on precipitation patterns and for the moderating effect they have on temperatures.

Urban climates

- Buildings interfere with both wind and air flow patterns and they change temperature regimes.
- In the high-rise cities of the world wind is channelled down streets.
- This **venturi effect** causes massive wind turbulence in city streets, particularly at night and especially in winter.
- Cities tend to have lower humidity rates, because of a lack of vegetation.
- Evaporation tends to be high, combined with turbulence; thunderstorms over or near cities are common.
- Increased light precipitation over and around cities is an observable feature, and may contrast markedly to the surrounding countryside.

Heat island effect

- Temperatures recorded over cities are usually one or two degrees higher than the surrounding countryside.
- If plotted on an isotherm map, temperatures show a marked decline from the central area to the edge of the city.
- Contributing factors are:
  - industry
  - central heating
  - heat retaining and emitting fabric of buildings
  - pollution blanket.

Examiner's Tip

AS structured questions frequently draw on these small 'sub-sections' of meteorology for questions.

Progress check

1 What are the differences between weather and climate?

2 Outline how the tri-cellular nature of the Earth's atmosphere produces the key features of the global climate.

3 Confusion about lapse rates can lead to confusion and frustration over the process of stability and instability in the atmosphere. There is no easy way to remember this concept!

Provide sentences that define fully:
- Relative humidity
- Environmental lapse rate
- Dry adiabatic lapse rate
- Saturated adiabatic lapse rate
- Stability
- Instability.

Now learn them!

4 What are the 'weather effects' of high and low pressure in Great Britain?

5 List the causes and consequences of tropical cyclones.

6 How does the weather affect our daily lives and economy?

7 The atmosphere is able to regulate the amount of insolation reaching the Earth's surface. How have we changed and affected this system?

8 How do urban areas affect climate?

Answers on page 89

Soils and ecosystems

Soil formation

- Soil is a vital, but often forgotten, finite resource.
- It is a residual layer of weathered material that has accumulated over a long period; this layer is sometimes known as the **regolith**.
- Geographers regard soil as an ecosystem, it has all the major functioning components of a dynamic ecosystem.
- The principle components of the soil system are water (25%), mineral matter (45%), air (25%), organic material/biota (5%).
- Parent material, climate, relief and time, also play significant roles.

The role of water

- *Transformation* of both the chemical composition and form of soil materials is due to water.
- Water breaks down and transforms litter into humus and is of major importance in transforming the mineral fraction through weathering.
- *Solution* takes place in the CO_2-rich atmosphere of the soil.
- *Hydration* occurs when minerals react in the presence of water by destroying crystal structures.
- *Hydrolysis* is the breakdown of minerals by hydrogen and hydroxyl ions derived from water.
- *Oxidation* and *reduction* also contribute to soil formation.
- *Transfers* within the soil are also performed by water. Water is stored temporarily in soil pores and plays a role in vertical (upwards and downwards) and lateral movements (on slopes) in the soil.
- *The principle pedogenetic processes* are a mix of transformations and transfers.

The principle transfers in the soil

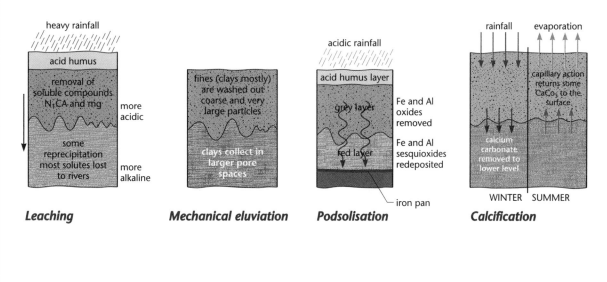

Leaching   **Mechanical eluviation**   **Podsolisation**   **Calcification**

Examiner's Tip

Clearly climate is the single most important pedogenic process at work in the above transfers.

(Continued next page)

Soil formation

The role of organic matter

- *Humus* is the remains of decomposed soil fauna and flora, organic matter.
- It is found in the upper parts of the A horizon and often has three distinct layers at different stages of decomposition, the **litter layer**, **fermentation layer** and **humification layer**.
- Different soils have different humus coverings, i.e. **mor** on acid soils and **mull** on alkaline soils.
- Organic material contributes nutrients to the soil.
- *Clay-humus molecules* are formed when clay and humus particles unite to form negatively charged molecules which attract positively charged plant food in the soil.

The role of mineral matter

- *Abiotic substances* (mineral matter) are the largest part of most soils.
- *Soil-particle size* relates to mineral matter.
- Three mineral fractions are identified based on the diameter sizes of particles, sand (2–0.05 mm), silt (0.05–0.002 mm) and clay (less than 0.002 mm).
- *Soil texture* is determined by the proportions of sand, silt and clay and this can be represented as a **soil texture triangle**.
- *Clay* is the most important fraction because it is chemically active.
- Clay particles are colloidal, they carry a negative charge and so repel one another.
- *Flocculation* describes clay particles when they finally come together.
- Flocculation can be accelerated, by adding lime or manure, to improve aeration and drainage.
- *Soil structure* is determined by the arrangement of mineral matter.
- *Peds* are formed when soil particles cling together, or aggregate.
- Peds contain both plant nutrients and allow for aeration and drainage.
- Peds occur in five key shapes (see below).

Appearance of aggregates (peds)					
Type of structure	Crumb	Platy	Blocky	Prismatic	Columnar

Soil classification

- Soils are classified into three main groups, azonal, intra-zonal and zonal.
- *Azonal soils* have developed recently and horizon development is poor, e.g. volcanic and alluvial soils.
- *Intra-zonal soils* are strongly influenced by parent material, e.g. rendzinas from calcium carbonate.
- *Zonal soils* are associated with specific climate and vegetation.

Examiner's Tip

It is the zonal soils that you will need to learn for the AS Level examination!

Four zonal soils

Podsol

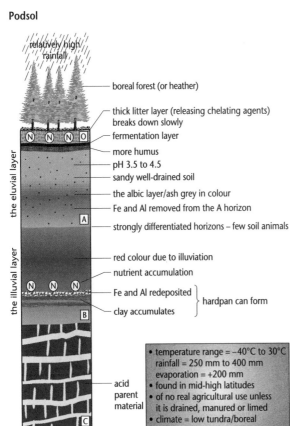

relatively high rainfall

boreal forest (or heather)

thick litter layer (releasing chelating agents) breaks down slowly

fermentation layer

more humus

pH 3.5 to 4.5

sandy well-drained soil

the albic layer/ash grey in colour

Fe and Al removed from the A horizon

strongly differentiated horizons – few soil animals

the eluvial layer

red colour due to illuviation

nutrient accumulation

Fe and Al redeposited } hardpan can form

clay accumulates

the illuvial layer

acid parent material

- temperature range = –40°C to 30°C rainfall = 250 mm to 400 mm evaporation = +200 mm
- found in mid-high latitudes
- of no real agricultural use unless it is drained, manured or limed
- climate = low tundra/boreal

Brown earth

moderate rainfall

deciduous woodland

litter layer

humus incorporated rapidly

light grey and very porous

worms and other soil animals mix soil and minerals in soil. There are poorly defined horizons in this soil

well drained

nutrients well distributed

pH 5 to 5.5

grading through red to brown in colour depending on mix of soil minerals

Ca and Mg removal accelerates

parent material

- temperature range = –5°C to 30°C rainfall = over 300 mm evaporation = +300 mm
- found in mid latitudes
- used extensively for agriculture
- climate = humid temperate

Chernozem

temperate grassland

grass litter

mull humus

fauna mix upper layers of A horizon giving rich dark brown/black colour

capillary rising enhances calcification (in summer)

increasing alkalinity

limited breakdown of organic inputs lower in the horizon

there is often no discernible A/B horizon

calcic layer (illuviation)

nodules of lime CaCo₃

soil biota active

krotovinas (burrows)

- temperature range = –5°C to 25°C rainfall = 200 mm to 500 mm evaporation = +800 mm
- found in lower-mid latitudes
- very fertile agricultural soil
- climate = temperate semi-arid

lime – rich parent material

Tropical soil

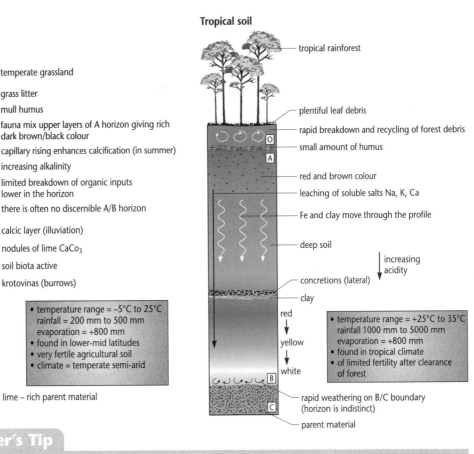

tropical rainforest

plentiful leaf debris

rapid breakdown and recycling of forest debris

small amount of humus

red and brown colour

leaching of soluble salts Na, K, Ca

Fe and clay move through the profile

deep soil

increasing acidity

concretions (lateral)

clay

red
↓
yellow
↓
white

- temperature range = +25°C to 35°C rainfall 1000 mm to 5000 mm evaporation = +800 mm
- found in tropical climate
- of limited fertility after clearance of forest

rapid weathering on B/C boundary (horizon is indistinct)

parent material

Examiner's Tip

It is important you learn the above profiles and link them with the vegetation and climatic types, on next page.

Links between soils, vegetation and climate

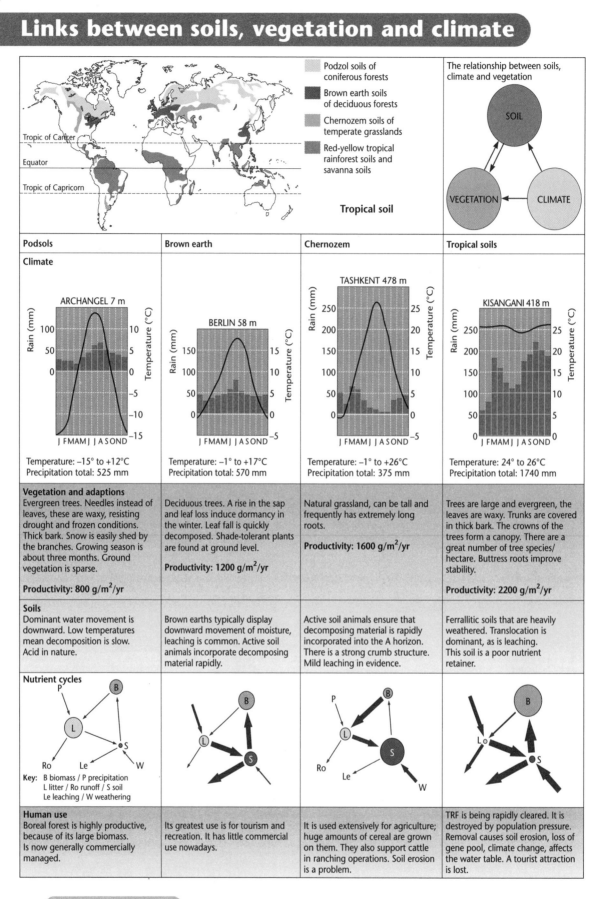

Podsols	**Brown earth**	**Chernozem**	**Tropical soils**
Climate			
ARCHANGEL 7 m Temperature: –15° to +12°C Precipitation total: 525 mm	**BERLIN 58 m** Temperature: –1° to +17°C Precipitation total: 570 mm	**TASHKENT 478 m** Temperature: –1° to +26°C Precipitation total: 375 mm	**KISANGANI 418 m** Temperature: 24° to 26°C Precipitation total: 1740 mm
Vegetation and adaptions Evergreen trees. Needles instead of leaves, these are waxy, resisting drought and frozen conditions. Thick bark. Snow is easily shed by the branches. Growing season is about three months. Ground vegetation is sparse. **Productivity: 800 g/m²/yr**	Deciduous trees. A rise in the sap and leaf loss induce dormancy in the winter. Leaf fall is quickly decomposed. Shade-tolerant plants are found at ground level. **Productivity: 1200 g/m²/yr**	Natural grassland, can be tall and frequently has extremely long roots. **Productivity: 1600 g/m²/yr**	Trees are large and evergreen, the leaves are waxy. Trunks are covered in thick bark. The crowns of the trees form a canopy. There are a great number of tree species/ hectare. Buttress roots improve stability. **Productivity: 2200 g/m²/yr**
Soils Dominant water movement is downward. Low temperatures mean decomposition is slow. Acid in nature.	Brown earths typically display downward movement of moisture, leaching is common. Active soil animals incorporate decomposing material rapidly.	Active soil animals ensure that decomposing material is rapidly incorporated into the A horizon. There is a strong crumb structure. Mild leaching in evidence.	Ferrallitic soils that are heavily weathered. Translocation is dominant, as is leaching. This soil is a poor nutrient retainer.
Nutrient cycles **Key:** B biomass / P precipitation L litter / Ro runoff / S soil Le leaching / W weathering			
Human use Boreal forest is highly productive, because of its large biomass. Is now generally commercially managed.	Its greatest use is for tourism and recreation. It has little commercial use nowadays.	It is used extensively for agriculture; huge amounts of cereal are grown on them. They also support cattle in ranching operations. Soil erosion is a problem.	TRF is being rapidly cleared. It is destroyed by population pressure. Removal causes soil erosion, loss of gene pool, climate change, affects the water table. A tourist attraction is lost.

Examiner's Tip

Realising that soils, vegetation and climate are inextricably linked is vital. AS Level looks frequently at this relationship.

Catenas

- Soil development is often related to the shape, lie and aspect of the land.
- Regular sequences of soil occur on slopes, catenas.
- *Podsols* typically form on the well-drained upper slopes.
- *Brown earths* form in the intermediate central area.
- *Gleys* form on the water-logged slope foot.

Soil management

- *Misuse of soil* on the whole reflects failure to understand and manage it.
- *Soil erosion* results from misuse, the accelerated process of natural landscape evolution!
- Soil erosion directly relates to overgrazing, intensive cultivation and deforestation, but is only part of the problem.
- *Soil degradation* is much more serious, involving misuse but also fertility decline.
- *Soil management* involves introducing techniques which maintain productivity without causing environmental damage.
- *Techniques* to cure accelerated soil erosion include:
  - intercropping
  - leaving crop residues in place after harvesting
  - improving and maintaining soil structure to limit removal by water and wind
  - introducing physical measures, such as windbreaks, shelter belts or terracing
  - using appropriate crop practices
  - planning careful future use of fertilisers
  - limiting, where feasible, deforestation
  - implementing appropriate agriculture and agricultural techniques.

Functions of ecosystems

- An ecosystem is composed of living and non-living components interacting to produce a stable system.

Cycling of energy

This is the most obvious process in the interactive ecosystem.
- Energy can be created, destroyed and transferred.
- Primary production via photosynthesis fixes energy from the sun into plants.
- The rate of energy fixing is expressed in $kg/m^2/year$ (or equivalent), and is fixed either as GPP (gross primary production) or as NPP (Net primary production).
- Energy is lost/released through respiration in the photosynthetic process.

Food chains

- Energy is moved or transferred in food chains.
- *Trophic levels* are the stages of energy exchange.
- Few food chains have more than five trophic levels because of this energy loss or exchange.
- Numbers of individuals, biomass and productivity decrease as trophic level four and five are reached.
- *Food webs* are a more realistic way to display energy flows.

Examiner's Tip

Because ecosystems are holistic, changes at one level often have far-reaching and unforeseen consequences in other parts of the system.

(Continued next page)

Functions of ecosystems

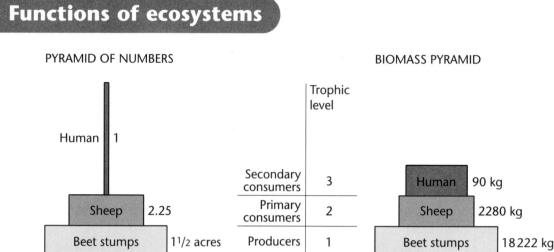

PYRAMID OF NUMBERS

BIOMASS PYRAMID

		Trophic level		
Human	1			
		Secondary consumers	3	Human	90 kg
Sheep	2.25	Primary consumers	2	Sheep	2280 kg
Beet stumps	1½ acres	Producers	1	Beet stumps	18 222 kg

Nutrient cycling

- This is the second of the processes in an ecosystem.
- It involves moving chemical elements out of the environment to organisms and then back again to the environment.
- Nutrients are stored in compartments and are recycled via pathways, see the diagram below:

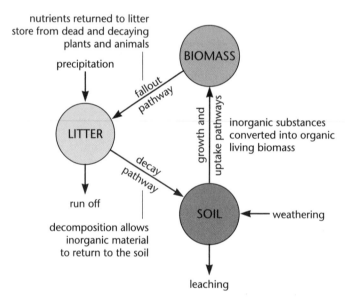

nutrients returned to litter store from dead and decaying plants and animals

precipitation

BIOMASS

fallout pathway

LITTER

growth and uptake pathways

inorganic substances converted into organic living biomass

decay pathway

run off

SOIL

weathering

decomposition allows inorganic material to return to the soil

leaching

- Stores are not static: nutrient amounts increase or decrease, store sizes vary. (N.B. They can be drawn any shape!)
- Humans can affect the cycling of nutrients in ecosystems by misusing or overusing the land.

Examiner's Tip

It is important that you are aware of a range of different nutrient cycles, for differing ecosystems. They appear frequently at AS Level.

Biomes: the distribution of vegetation on a global scale

- There is a very close link/relationship between climates, soil and vegetation.
- This zonal relationship can be explained using the concept of the biome (named after the vegetation found within a zone).
- Four factors determine biomal distribution: soil, relief, biota and climate. (Refer back to the table on page 26.)

Broadleaf temperate deciduous forest (BTDF)

- In the world as a whole, 19% of the biomass by biome is BTDF.
- Present plant species in the UK BTDF date mainly from the last ice-age.
- Since their first appearance in the UK BTDF has been markedly depleted, especially near the major cities.
- *Characteristics* of BTDF are:
  - leaf loss, a form of dormancy in response to the cold winter months when there is little soil water and low sunlight/energy
  - a growing season of about seven months
  - extreme sensitivity to temperature changes
  - a definite tree line, above which they will not grow.
  - Principal soils of the BTDF are the brown earths.
- *Uses* of BTDF include game management, timber production, as shelter-belts and recreation.
- Most conservationists would advocate that this multi-purpose use is, if managed properly, the best way to use BTDF.
- *Forest Enterprise* was one of the 'branches' that came out of the Forestry Commission split in 1992.
- Its mission is to develop and maintain attractive and productive woodlands.

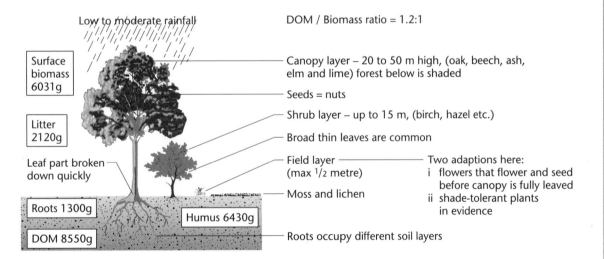

A section through the BTDF

Examiner's Tip

A knowledge and understanding of a range of small-scale (BTDFs) and larger-scale (TRFs) is a requirement of many specifications at AS Level.

Succession and climax

- Ecosystems are dynamic and continually evolving.
- **Succession** is the predictable pattern of vegetational change.
- **Prisere** is the term for the chain of vegetational changes.
- **Sere** is the term for each successive stage.
- Each stage is an advance on the previous one offering increased protection and shelter, better soil conditions and an increased nutrient stock for the plants that follow.
- Colonisation is the process whereby the first, **pioneer species** invade the soil.
- **Climax** is the ultimate stage when vegetation is mature and the ecosystem is fully developed. (If there is a link between climate and the final form of the vegetation it is called a climatic climax community).

Four types of succession/prisere exist.

- Xeroseres are successions in dry conditions; the **lithosere** (on rock) and **psammosere** (on sand).
- Hydroseres are successions in water: the **hydrosere** (in freshwater) and the **halosere** (in salt water).

A dune ecosystem

- Ynyslas Dunes in West Wales are a typical example of a psammosere.

How Ynyslas Dunes formed

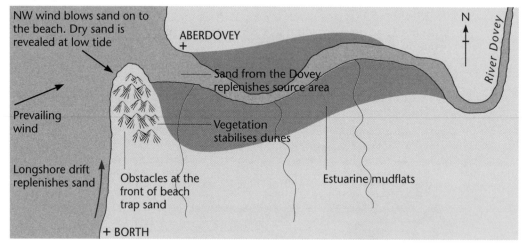

The dune succession

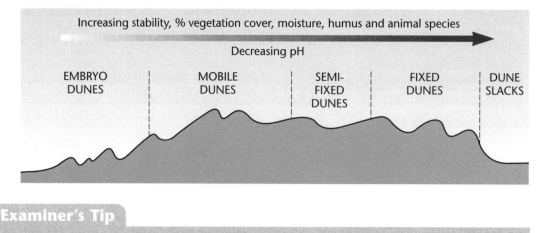

Examiner's Tip

Remember that progression through an ecological succession increases biomass, biodiversity and productivity.

Embryo dunes

- These are an extremely difficult environment.
- Sand is dry, lacking in nutrients, there is poor water retention, high alkaline pH and salt spray, and immersion in salt water are problems.
- Pioneer plants, e.g. Sea Rocket and Sea Couch are important in slowing wind erosion but have to be **xerophytic** (drought tolerant) and **halophytic** (salt tolerant).
- Few animals colonize embryo dunes.

Mobile Dunes

- These move and change because of the effects of wind.
- Marram grass is the dominant vegetational type as it is tolerant of the extremely dry conditions.
- It begins to stabilise the dunes permitting Groundsel and Sea Spurge to grow.
- There is still no real colonisation by animals.

Semi-fixed dunes

- Soils begin to develop so conditions for plants are better.
- Mosses and lichens start to colonise the area followed by a range of flowering plants assisted by increased nitrogen fixation.
- Animals are common, from rabbits through to invertebrates.

Fixed Dunes

- These are the most stable of the dunes and are covered in vegetation.
- Plant growth at its maximum as conditions are ideal.
- Humus incorporation into the soil begins.

Dune slacks

- These are hollows formed by erosion by wind until the water table is revealed. They can be rich in different varieties of vegetation.

Management of ecosystems at a local scale: dunes

- Dunes perform an important role in protecting the coastline.
- Dune soils and vegetation are fragile: vulnerable to the trampling of humans and burrowing and grazing of rabbits and other animals.
- If the thin mantle of regolith is damaged and sand revealed, this can lead to **blowouts**, massive deflation hollows on dune crests.
- Management techniques include:
  - moveable board walks, zig-zagged to deter motorbikes and other vehicles
  - low fencing to deter 'wanderers' and to funnel visitors
  - advice boards and direction arrows to help visitors make the most of their tour
  - wardens, tolls and admission fees to control numbers of visitors
  - designated car parking
  - 'sacrificing' small areas to visitors to protect others
  - culling, poisoning and shooting animal invaders.

Examiner's Tip

Remember the term **plagioclimax**; this is vegetation which owes its characteristics to human activity (e.g. heather moorland). We hold many areas of the world in plagioclimax, to enable agricultural activity to occur.

Management of ecosystems at a global scale: tropical rainforest

- The world's tropical rainforests (TRF) are delicate and important to people, and their destruction has global consequences.
- TRF deteriorates at a phenomenal rate when interfered with.
- At present the top ten countries lose rainforest at the rate of 3000 to 35 000 km²/yr, that is 1.5% of total forest area per year.
- It is cleared for a variety of reasons: to allow access to minerals, for HEP production, to allow cultivation, for cattle ranching, and for timber, for paper, furniture and energy.

Impacts of deforestation

Plants and animals
- Soils become nutrient impoverished as the nutrient cycle is breached.
- Species are lost and the genetic stock/potential is lost.
- Niches are lost.
- Fertile soil is lost.
- Seeds fail to germinate.

The water cycle
- Greater sediment load causes silting and flooding.
- Runoff increases when vegetation cover is damaged.
- Water quality is affected.

Landscape
- Soil is lost.
- Gullying and sheet wash is more common.
- Duricrust forms an infertile hardpan.

Climate
- Carbon release to the atmosphere accelerates global warming.
- Rainfall starts to decrease.
- Humidity drops.
- Changes occur in daily temperatures.
- Albedo effects on bare soil.

Population
- Indigenous people lose their homes and way of life.
- Exposure to outside influences allows disease to spread.

Sustainable use of the tropical rainforest system

TRF can be managed to meet the needs of plants and animals, indigenous populations and to contribute to the economic development of countries (see below).

Sustainable management

- Create biosphere reserves (a UNESCO idea) with zones for settlement and research.
- Develop eco-tourism.
- Introduce alternative technology, i.e. biomass instead of wood.
- Replant cleared areas with fast growing 'nursery' trees.
- Leave fruiting trees as an animal food source.
- Don't log riverside trees. Set limits for yields.
- 'Police' felling.
- Educate people to understand conservation.
- Resettle indigenous tribes.
- Develop 'debt for nature' ideas.

Examiner's Tip

Definition: In terms of the TRF, sustainability is where the needs of plants, animals and indigenous populations are met whilst GNP continues to grow.

Progress check

1 (a) Draw a labelled cross section through a podsol, to show the horizons.

   (b) Explain the importance of climate and vegetation in the formation of podsols.

   (c) How can man make such soils suitable for agricultural purposes?

2 Describe and explain the process of soil formation that characteristically occurs in temperate and tropical areas.

3 Outline the differences and similarities between podsolisation, leaching, calcification and eluviation.

4 (a) Soil study 'in the field' usually involves an assessment of soil texture, soil structure, soil acidity and organic content. How is each of these assessments undertaken?

   (b) How do soil features and characteristics vary along a catena or valley transect?

5 For either the TRF or BDTF outline how climate, soils and vegetation affect and link one to another.

6 (a) For the psammosere/dune ecosystem draw a diagram to illustrate how the succession of vegetation leads to the climax stage.

   (b) How does primary succession vary from secondary succession?

   (c) Ecosystems can be changed by human activity. Outline how man can affect the climatic climax community.

7 (a) How does deforestation impact the TRF?

   (b) Why does the use of the TRF have to be sustainably based?

Answers on page 90

Hydrology

Rivers as systems

- Rivers dominate the physical landscape, producing widespread changes.
- Rivers remove rock and material from mass wasting, particularly, but not exclusively in the humid areas of the world.
- Rivers move under gravity in a channel transferring both water and sediment downstream.
- Rivers act as open systems. Stores and transfers vary in size according to changes in inputs of water.
- *Dynamic equilibrium* means that all sections of the 'system' balance.

The hydrological cycle

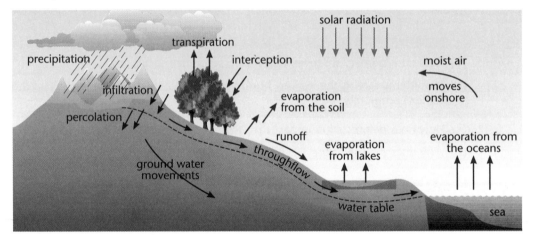

- The river represents the flow of water overland, but two key 'hidden' aspects, infiltration and ground water, are of vital significance.

Infiltration

- The fundamental part of the drainage basin system, contributing to groundwater storage, throughflow and stream channel recharge.

Infiltration rates are affected by a number of factors, including:

- *The nature of precipitation*: its duration, total, the area covered, the size of raindrops, frequency and its chemical composition.
- *Vegetation interception* which depends on the nature of the vegetation, e.g. pine forests takes out 96% of low intensity rainfall leaving only 4% to infiltrate.
- *The effect of depression storage*, the geological structure and man's agricultural activity. Water captured in the landscape, or plough-furrows infiltrates!
- *Evapotranspiration* – available heat, wind, and the texture and depth of soils affect how much water returns to the atmosphere from exposed water surfaces and from vegetation.
- *The nature of the soils*, their permeability, porosity and texture.
- *Slope length and angle* determine whether runoff or infiltration is the dominant process.

Examiner's Tip

Questions on the hydrological cycle are central to the study of hydrology. But do ensure that you write what the question wants. Answers offered by candidates on the hydrological cycle are frequently too involved and miss the point of the question.

Groundwater

- This appears and collects in permeable rocks, known as aquifers which are saturated as a result of infiltration by rainfall.
- Water flows between the small grains of rock and soil that make up the aquifer.
- Variations in the shape of the water table reflect the surface topography; that is, the water table is near the surface in valleys and deep down in the hills.
- It is because of the topography of the landscape the groundwater 'flows'.
- The velocity of flow is proportional to the hydraulic gradient (simply the slope of the water table induced by the topography of the landscape).
- Speeds are typically between 1m/yr to 1m/day.
- Most rivers gain their water/flow from a combination of surface runoff and groundwater discharge.
- Groundwater contributes most water in summer and autumn in the UK, surface runoff contributing in the wetter winter and spring months.

River energy

- River channels not only transfer water and sediment.
- The potential and kinetic energy within the water does the work of erosion, transportation and deposition within the river.
- Flow type affects the efficiency of a river to erode, transport or deposit.
- Two principle flow types are recognised, **turbulent flow** and **laminar flow**. Both are affected by friction.

Energy flow relationships

- During periods of low flow, below bank stage flow or when rivers are at base flow low energy conditions are experienced and little 'work' is done.
- Channel adjustments are most likely to occur during the rising phase of the storm hydrograph, when there is a lot of water in the system and erosion is at its height.
- Deposition occurs as discharge and energy declines on the falling limb of the storm hydrograph.
- A relationship exists between volume and velocity and individual particle erosion, transportation and deposition; this is displayed on the **Hjulström Curve**

Examiner's Tip

Process questions are often used at AS Level to confirm your participation in practical fieldwork.

HYDROLOGY

Erosion

- To understand the important work that erosion does in a river three areas have to be further explored, volume, velocity and load.

Volume

- Most streams and rivers obtain their water from rainfall or any of the other forms of precipitation.
- This precipitation either evaporates, percolates or infiltrates, or contributes to the runoff or drainage of the land surface.
- As these rivers flow from high (source areas) to lower areas (the mouth) their volume increases as contributions from other parts of the drainage basin and via tributaries are added.
- There can be variations in a rivers volume, these relate to seasonality of rainfall (in monsoon areas), the contribution of snow melt and of springs and groundwater.
- *Discharge* (Q) is defined as the volume of water passing a particular point in a river in a unit of time.
- It is expressed as m^3/s^{-1}, or in cumecs
  ($Q = AV$: where A = cross-sectional area and V = velocity).

Velocity

- Velocity is more or less constant along the length of the river as competing factors cancel each other.
- Steeper slopes do encourage higher velocities, but this is decreased as a result of friction.
- Larger channels of the lower course exert less friction than the small channels of the upper course, allowing the river to become more efficient.

Load

- The volume of water carried + the velocity of this water = energy of the river.
- Energy availability determines the capacity (total load) and calibre (the weight/size dimensions of individual particles).
- Small streams carry a greater quantity of fine material than of coarse.
- Large rivers with more available energy carry larger/coarser material.
- The *erosive power of a river is for the most part determined by the 'charge' of debris it carries. Running water has restricted erosional ability*.
- However, with increased load a river is more likely to begin to aggrade, or deposit.

Mechanisms of erosion

- *Entrained material* refers to particles removed from the bed and banks of the river by erosion and used in the erosional process.
- This entrained material is acquired in three ways. By:
  - *vertical erosion* which deepens channels
  - *lateral erosion* which increases a rivers width
  - *headward erosion* which increases the length of a river by cutting back the point of origin in the source area.

Corrasion and attrition

- These two processes rely upon the load of the river to achieve their effects.
- Both processes occur most often during periods of higher river flow.

Examiner's Tip

Don't forget the contribution that Hjulström made to our understanding of fluvial velocity and a river's ability to either erode, transport or deposit.

- The debris that results from the corrasive processes is free to collide and bash into itself, this process known as attrition (or **communition**) causes a reduction in particle size in a downstream direction.

Hydraulic action
- Most effective in the middle and lower courses, where the bed and banks are likely to be composed of incoherent sediments.
- *Cavitation* is an extreme form of hydraulic action when the sudden and violent collapse of bubbles created by this process shatters banks extremely rapidly.

Transport

Essential conditions for movement
- Resisting forces have to be overcome.
- *Critical tractive force* must be present, e.g. drag must exceed particle inertia.
- *Competent velocity* has to be achieved, the lowest velocity at which particles of a particular size are set in motion (the bigger the particle the greater the velocity needed to move it).

Methods of sediment transport in rivers
- *Traction* – boulders and rocks are rolled along the bed.
- *Suspension* – particles are held in the body of the water.
- *Solution* – material is dissolved in the water.
- *Saltation* – particles are bounced along the bottom.

Downstream changes in sediment
- Amounts of material moved increase in a downstream direction, as weathered material is input and as tributaries add material.
- Material gets progressively smaller and rounder on its journey downstream.

Deposition

- Depositional processes occur when the **carrying capacity** of a river is reduced.
- Factors which affect the capacity of a river to retain its transported load include:
  - *Water velocity changes* due to changes in gradient, or a break in slope, usually caused by variations in geology.
  - *Geology*, can by changing the chemical composition of river water cause rapid vegetational growth, this slows water and causes deposition.
  - *Evaporation* (as on the Nile) or *over-abstraction* (as on the Colorado) can reduce flow and consequently bring on deposition.
  - *Additional debris and water volume from tributaries* can result in the slowing down of water and to deposition.
- Thus deposition is not confined to the lower reaches of rivers: it can occur at almost any point along the river's course.
- Localised deposition can, during periods of high flow, cause local flooding.

Examiner's Tip

It should be obvious that the effects of erosion, transportation and deposition determine the landforms that form in fluvial systems.

Fluvial features

The graded profile or profile of equilibrium

- Different parts or sub-sections of a river's course have different characteristics.

The graded profile

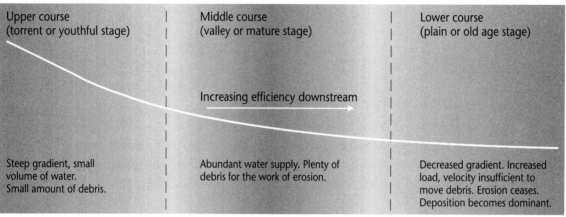

Upper course (torrent or youthful stage)	Middle course (valley or mature stage)	Lower course (plain or old age stage)
	Increasing efficiency downstream	
Steep gradient, small volume of water. Small amount of debris.	Abundant water supply. Plenty of debris for the work of erosion.	Decreased gradient. Increased load, velocity insufficient to move debris. Erosion ceases. Deposition becomes dominant.

- The graded profile or state of equilibrium is thus achieved when river's course is as efficient as it can be from source to mouth.
- In practice, a river course is rarely graded as changes in rock type and sea level ensure the profile is constantly changing.
- Variation in gradient, volume of water and amount of debris lead to the development of characteristic landforms for each stage of the river.

The upper course

Features are many and include:

- *Interlocking spurs*, e.g. River Dane, Derbyshire.
- *Potholes* where pebbles and debris swirl around in joints and hollows on the river bed, gradually drilling a hole in the river bed, e.g. River Taff, Glamorgan.
- *Waterfalls and rapids* where there is a variety of different strength rocks, steeper gradients and fast water.
- *Gorges* where, over the course of time, waterfalls and rapids migrate upstream forming dramatic transverse profiles.

The middle course

- The change in the shape and size of the valley is due to the way water flows through meanders (see diagram opposite).

Meanders

- Erosion occurs on concave banks, deposition on convex banks and slowly the meander moves downstream.
- There is speculation over how they originally form but obstructions are an unlikely cause.
- Meanders may or may not be attempting to release excess energy from the river system, e.g. River Ribble, Lancashire; River Yare, Norfolk.
- Meanders continue to grow in size: the floodplain gets bigger and bluffs are cut.
- When the river floods it leaves material (deposits) over a floodplain.

Examiner's Tip

Don't forget about the effects rejuvenation has on the graded profile, i.e. knick points, waterfalls, rapids and river terraces. Be able to draw annotated diagrams of these landforms.

Cross-section through a meander

A ... fastest thread of water ... corkscrew motion of river water ... B

river cliff

water thrown to outside bank by centripetal forces

bubbles release material in the bank

helicoidal flow causes cavitation on outside bank

THALWEG

outside bank gradually undercut and then it collapses

pool (deep water)

asymmetrical shape to channel

point bar/slip off slope

sediment layers indicate different periods of deposition

← surface flow
←--- subsurface flow

The lower course

Features are many and include:

Ox-bow lakes

- As meanders grow in size they can breach their banks.
- When this happens a cut-off/mort lake or ox-bow forms, e.g. Mort Lake, London and the Trent Valley, Nottinghamshire.

Braiding

- Occurs when a river flows or moves through a series of interlocking channels, rather than through a single thread.
- They are thought to form because of load v discharge differences, induced by changes in slope and additions of water from tributaries/floods.
- They are highly unstable as the river is trying to achieve a more efficient profile.

Deltas

- The biggest of the world's rivers reach the sea, a lake or a lagoon with a massive load of material.
- This debris is dropped into the calmer water of the receiving areas.
- Salty water encourages debris to flocculate.
- The shallow angle of the coastal strip encourages deposition.
- Three main types of delta exist:
  - *arcuate*, e.g. The Mekong Delta, SE Asia
  - *birds foot*, e.g. the Mississippi Delta, USA
  - *estuarine*, e.g. the Seine Delta, France.

Floodplain

- Lands susceptible to flooding.
- Widened by meander migration.
- Edge of floodplain is marked by bluffs.

Examiner's Tip

It is vital that you are able to draw diagrams to support your knowledge of fluvial landforms.

Variable regimes in rivers

- The regime of a river refers to variations in discharge that occur seasonally.
- Regimes are affected by climate.
- Tropical/equatorial climates may exhibit regular or simple cycles.
- Seasonal temperate climates of Western Europe have more complex regimes with 'multiple' peaks, affected variably by snow/glacial melt, rainfall and evapotranspiration.

Measuring regimes: hydrographs

- For single storm/precipitation events the relationship between precipitation and discharge are shown on a **storm hydrograph**.
- The appearance and labelling of the hydrograph is shown below.
- Physical factors in the drainage basin can affect its shape, i.e.:
  - The nature of the inputs, principally precipitation
  - The characteristics of the catchment area, basin size and shape, rock type, relief and deforestation/afforestation.

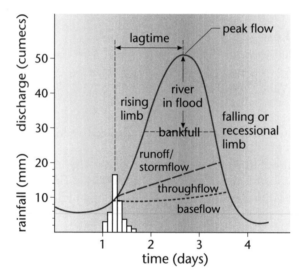

How human activity affects the hydrographs

These are numerous and have direct and indirect effects upon the hydrology of a basin and the hydrograph.

- *Land drainage* affects the input of water to a river channel.
- *The storing of water in reservoirs* increases evaporation and regulates discharge.
- *Deforestation* decreases interceptional evotranspiration, increases outland flow and changes patterns of throughput.
- *Urbanisation* creates impervious tarmac surfaces preventing infiltration, increasing overland flow and resulting in shorter lag times and higher discharges.
- *Irrigation and water abstraction induce* long-term changes in groundwater supplies.

Floods

- Floods are the most important aspect of river flow.
- When rivers are in flood they have the greatest energy, changing the landscape dramatically.
- Floods affect man: they destroy property and crops, and kill!
- In the UK floods are relatively uncommon, recurring as they do every two to four years.
- They generally result from a coincidental combination of a number of factors or conditions (i.e. dry/bare ground and torrential rain).
- Most serious flooding results from man's occupation of low-lying land in the belief that protective measures will be effective.
- Small basins are especially prone to **flash flooding** which accounts for 80% of lives lost to drowning.

Flood prediction

Hydrologists use three main approaches:

- *flood magnitude analysis* based on measured characteristics, on flood hydrographs
- *recurrence interval calculations* based on computer-stored records and statistical forecasting (recurrence is to do with the interval between similar-sized floods)
- *probability predictions*, useful but not reliable.

Human response to floods

Adjustments in actions on the floodplain

- none
- emergency action
- flood proofing
- land use regulation
- financial disincentives

Abatement of problems in the catchment

- afforestation
- change of vegetation use
- change agricultural practices
- affect of urban areas

Protection along the channel

- walls and embankments
- channel improvements
- diversion schemes
- reservoirs
- barrages and flood barriers

Water as a resource

- We can no longer take our water supply for granted.
- Most river systems are inherently robust (for instance, salmon have returned to the Thames), nevertheless rivers will increasingly need to be managed in a more sustainable way.
- Management involves both the present and the future.
- Geographers, biologists, environmental scientists, engineers and politicians will need to work together to ensure water supply for our consumption, industrial and agricultural use.
- Man will have to interfere in the hydrological cycle, to supply water for our growing populations.
- We will have to reconsider our occupancy of the floodplain.
- We have to control the excesses that occur in rivers and maintain and regulate flow to ensure water quality, to allow for transport and leisure, and to maintain and enhance the landscape.

Examiner's Tip

You should realise that floods result from both natural processes and human activities.

Management issues

Environmental solutions to flooding

- Since the end of the nineteenth century we have 'trained' rivers, mostly to control flooding.
- Such training is expensive, extensive and unnecessarily manipulative.
- This area of management has seen the most promising of reforms over the last decade.
  - *Pools, riffles and meanders are now reconstructed*, as they are seen as the best, most stable alternative to artificial straightening.
  - *The re-introduction of vegetation* is seen as important, as it duplicates and promotes the bank stability of the natural stream channel.
  - *Stream maintenance*, which is small scale and in harmony with the watery environment is seen as important.
  - *Bio-technical methods* copy and reproduce the natural symmetry/asymmetry of the stream channel.

Pollution control

- The flush toilet, and liquid waste from industry have both contributed to the deterioration of our water systems.
- Nitrates and herbicides (in the UK) have accelerated the problem in the last 25 years.
- Legislative development, spurred on by our involvement with Europe, has built apace in the last twenty years.
- Rivers are now cleaner than they have been for hundreds of years.

A future for groundwater?

- 200 years on we still rely on groundwater, as an economic source for our urbanised population.
- However, in some areas groundwater in the main aquifers is being depleted and polluted.
- Contamination from agricultural land, from landfill and from industrial seepage must be controlled, as must the maintenance of adequate river flows.
- Management of aquifers in the future to ensure effective supply and use for drinking water and as part of an integrated system using rivers, etc. will be paramount.

Disputes and dam building

- The disputes that surround dam construction are complex and involve environmental, economic and political factors.
- Most dams that are built tend to be multi-purpose, supplying energy, providing water for irrigation and allowing for recreation and leisure pursuits.
- Hydro-politics, or the management of water resources in shared basins is the most contentious of issues related to dam building at the present time.
- Interference with water, in an international river, always has a downstream effect that can lead to intense confrontation.

Water transfers

- Under the 1991 Water Resources Act, the Environment Agency must ensure that water resources are conserved, redistributed, augmented and properly used.
- One way that resource delivery has been improved is through schemes to transfer water, a costly option but one that will increasingly develop after some two decades of overbuilding of dams.

Examiner's Tip

There isn't an infinite amount of water in the world – we have to manage it. AS questions frequently focus on this topic.

Progress check

1 (a) On a flow diagram show the transfers and processes water goes through in the hydrological cycle.
   (b) What factors influence the infiltration capacity of the soil?

2 Explain how the term dynamic equilibrium relates to the concept of the graded profile.

3 Why are large streams better transporting agents than small streams?

4 Velocity is an important variable in particle transport. What contribution did Hjulström make to our understanding of sediment transport in rivers?

5 In what way do the features of the river channel vary from the river valley?

6 How can physical variations and the characteristics of the catchment basin affect the shape of the storm hydrograph? How can the flood hydrograph help hydrological engineers?

7 Floods are often the result of both physical and human factors. Outline some of the human factors.

Answers on page 90–91

Coasts

- The coast is constantly changing.
- As a high proportion of the world's population live near the coast we must deal with the threats and problems it poses to human habitation.
- Problems include: flooding, rising sea levels, accelerated erosion, the effects of industrial pollution and the effects of tourism.
- Careful, sustainable management of the coast helps to deal with these problems.
- The coastal environment is defined in geographical terms below:

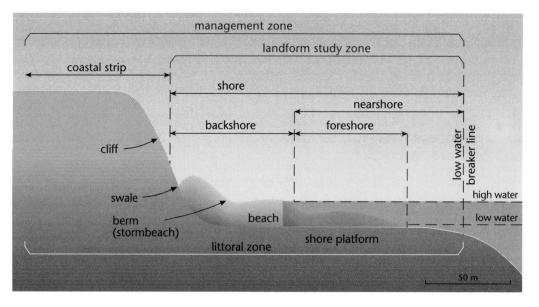

- Traditionally coastal geomorphologists have tried to classify the coast according to whether the dominant process is erosional or depositional.
- Currently the relationships between mechanisms and processes to landforms are again being explored, the so called 'process-landform response approach', below:

Inputs of energy →	Processes →	Landform response →	Outputs
Tides, wind and waves	Sediment transport	2d – beach (slope/shape)	of energy (breaking waves)
		3d – landforms (stacks/cliffs, etc.)	and sediment on the sea floor

Note: sediment transport is a coverall for erosion + deposition. There is no permanent loss of sediment, it is just moved back and forth.

Examiner's Tip

A knowledge of the above terms will be crucial to your understanding of the coastal system.

Shaping the coast

- The interaction between waves, tides and coastal currents shape, modify and mould the shoreline.
- All three can act against and work with one another.

Waves

- These provide the energy for the coastal system, they are the force behind the formation and shaping of the coast.
- The drag effects of wind across the sea causes undulations on the surface.
- As these undulations build (because of pressure contrasts on the windward and leeward sides) so water starts to move in an orbital or oscillatory fashion inside them. This is related to their height.
- Energy conversion, from potential to kinetic, occurs continually within these waves.
- Thus waves are a means of moving energy through water with only small displacements of water particles in the direction of energy flow.
- Remember: wave size is determined by the **fetch** (the distance over open water that the wind has blown) and the duration of the blow. N Norfolk has a fetch of 1500+ km.
- Waves that break can be either **constructive** or **destructive**. See diagram below:

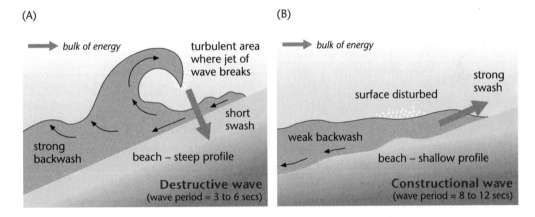

- Swash runs up the beach. Backwash runs down the beach.
- Four types of wave have been identified: surging, collapsing, plunging (in A) and spilling (as in B).
- As waves move nearer the coast the submarine contours/sea bed starts to affect the waves. Locally both friction and drag start to increase. This is known as wave refraction and has the effect of varying the available energy along a coastline.

Currents

- These spread and redistribute energy/sediment along the coastline.
- Shore-normal currents establish a cell circulation in the nearshore zone.
- A large amount of sediment is moved up the beach by the swash and is balanced by the rip of the backwash running back down the beach.
- The vast amount of water moving back down the beach forms a **riphead**, a deep (up to 3 m+) energy/water dissipation hollow offshore.
- The effect of the strong, sediment-laden swash is to form a beach **cusp**, the smallest of the beach depositional features.

Examiner's Tip

It is important to realise the link between the openness of the coast, the shape of submarine contours' beach angle, the wind's strength and duration and its effect on wave power.

(Continued next page)

Shaping the coast

Longshore drift

- For the most part waves approach coasts at a slight angle, less than 10° is normal.
- These wave-normal/oblique currents, aided by winds and submarine currents carry sediment up the beach at the same angle as the wave/current, and return it to the sea at right angles to the beach.
- The net effect is to move material along a beach.
- Waves approaching at 30° move most sediment along a shore!
- Most sediment on beaches has a river or offshore origin.
- Most sediment moves W to E in the UK. Along East Anglia's coasts it moves N to S.

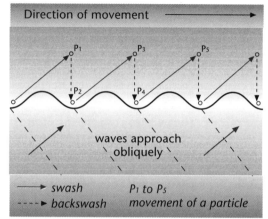

Direction of movement

waves approach
obliquely

→ swash
---→ backswash

P_1 to P_5
movement of a particle

Tides

- These spread energy over a large vertical area of the coast.
- Erosional processes are concentrated between high (HTM) and low tide (LTM) marks, in the splash zone above the HTM and the wave base below LTM.

Erosion

- Erosional processes work to destroy the coastline.

Quarrying (on hard rock coastlines), or **hydraulic action** (on soft rock coasts).

- The compression, as a wave hits a coast, and expansion as it retreats exerts considerable pressure on the coastline.

Abrasion/corrasion

- Waves use the pebbles and cobbles to corrade the cliff base, undercutting it rapidly.
- Weaknesses in rocks, joints, etc. are differentially exploited.

Attrition

- Reduces the size, and rounds off individual pebbles, as they bash into one another.

Sub-aerial weathering

Corrosion and solution

- The chemical dissolving of rock in acido-saline conditions.

Sea weathering

- A process called slaking, caused by the alternate wetting and drying of the coast, along with salt crystallization are most prevalent.

Biological weathering and bio-erosion

- The effects of boring plants and animals on the coast.

Mass-movement

- Rockfalls, mudslides, slumps and slides deliver material to the coastal sediment system.

Examiner's Tip

You must know your coastal processes for AS Level!

Erosional landforms

Cliffs

- Are probably the principal and most obvious feature on the coastline.
- They vary in height, orientation, steepness and in terms of their lithology and structure.
- Wave energy concentrates energy at the cliff base, forming a wave-cut notch, the size of which is determined by the tidal range.
- As time passes the overhanging cliff eventually collapses, this material is used as ammunition to accelerate the destruction of the wave-cut notch.
- A relationship between rock type, erosion and cliff morphology exists.

Shore platforms

- As shorelines, coastal slopes and cliff lines are eroded there is a marked/obvious retreat or recession that leaves behind a platform.
- These platforms have an overall convex shape and an average slope of 0° to 3°.
- Most show a break in slope, marking the LTM.
- Present-day processes have produced most platforms.

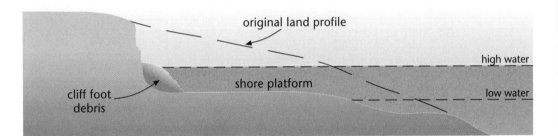

- For a long period of time a single process, abrasion, was held responsible for the formation of shore platforms.
- The modern view is that shore platforms have a multiple-process origin, a combination of:
  - *Abrasion* Sand grains moved by waves plane the platform surface (particularly in the upper shore section).
  - *Mechanical wave-erosion* Quarrying, through wave hammer, compression or pressure release, picks out and exploits variations in lithology, causing cliff recession and roughening the platform surface.
  - *Weathering* Wetting and drying can cause hydration and oxidation, and salt crystallisation.
  - *Subaerial processes: solution* Attacks calcareous rocks (limestone/chalk) especially in tropical areas, but even in Norfolk as slight rises or falls away from the atypical sea temperature produce rapid chemical stripping.
  - *Tides* vary the level of process activity.

Arches and stacks

- The sea erodes along a line of weakness (e.g. a fault) in a headland to form a cave.
- Caves formed on opposite sides of headlands join to form an arch, e.g. Durdle Door.
- The arch will eventually collapse to form a stack, e.g. Old Harry.

Examiner's Tip

It is important to be able to draw simple diagrams, similar to the shore-platform diagram above, for all coastal features.

(Continued next page)

Erosional landforms

Geos and blow-holes

- Where a fault in a cliff, at right angles to a coast is eroded by the sea, a long narrow inlet may form, e.g. Huntsman's Leap, Pembroke.
- The first stage may well be a cave, which connects to the surface by a chimney to form a blow-hole or gloup.

The variety of features on the Dorset coast

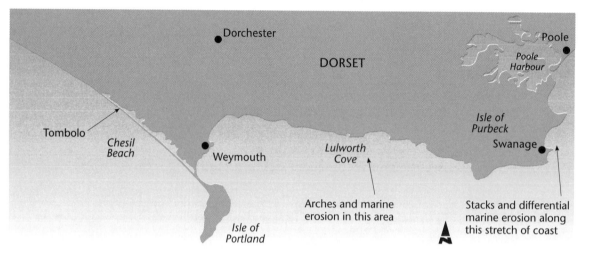

Landforms of coastal deposition

- The debris from coastal erosion is moved and deposited by waves and currents.

Beaches

- The most widespread of depositional landforms.
- Geomorphologically successful because of the mobility of their loose sand sediment.
- Landforms are the results of coast processes reworking beach sediments.
- These complex systems exhibit a range of minor landforms, below:

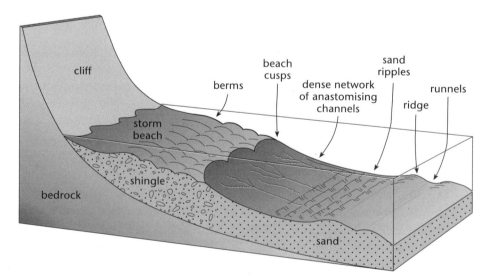

- Beaches are the best form of defence for a coastline (as they absorb energy).
- They are easily destroyed by natural and man-induced processes.
- Bars and spits are types of detached beach.

Bars

- Created by the action of breaking offshore waves on gently sloping shores.
- The breaking waves excavate material from the sea floor to form submarine bars, which slowly build up until they appear above SL and are frequently quickly vegetated.
- Bars frequently move onshore/inland; trapped sea water in the form of a lagoon is filled by sediment and marsh vegetation as at Looe, in Cornwall.
- The best examples of bars in the UK are found off the Norfolk Coast between Hunstanton and Sheringham, e.g. Scolt Head Island.

Spits

- Created for the most part by longshore drift, they are attached to the shore and end in deep water.
- Blakeney Point Spit may have formed from an offshore bar.

Features of Blakeney Spit

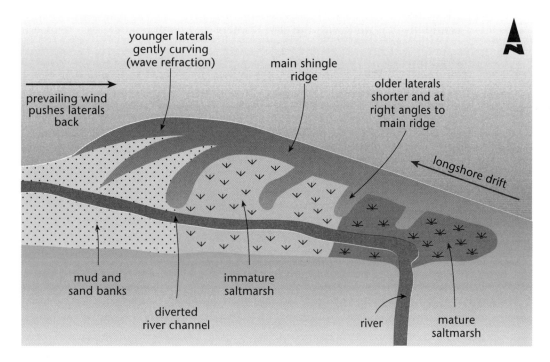

Tombolos

- Chesil Beach is a fine example of a tombolo.
  - It is a 30 km shingle ridge connecting the Isle of Portland to the mainland.
  - From West Bay to Abbotsbury it hugs the coast with an elongated lagoon, the Fleet, separating it from the mainland.
  - The beach is a simple ridge reaching a maximum size at Portland, where it is 60 m wide and 13 m high.
  - There is a progressive grading in the size of the material from pear-sized at West Bay to fist-sized at Portland.
  - Whether the beach is a spit or a bar driven ashore is not clear.

Cuspate forelands

- Cuspate forelands are spits that have been enlarged by the accretion of ridges parallel to their shores. A classic example is Dungeness Foreland.

Examiner's Tip

Knowing the sort of detail, as outlined on the above diagram, can save you hundreds of words!

Managing coasts

- 16.9 million of the UK's population lives within 10 km of the coast.
- Buildings, roads and recreation facilities occupy 31% of the coastal frontage of the UK.
- 40% of the UK's manufacturing industry is also situated on or near the coast.
- With so much of the coast developed or being developed, there is a demand for coastal protection from erosion, and sea and tidal defences against flooding.
- Coastal defences have to protect the population and their economic well being.
- Approximately 2100 km of coast defences presently defend our coastlines, mainly along the East and East Anglian coast.
- Management of our coastlines is the responsibility of Maritime Local District Councils, MAFF and the Environment Agency (and other groups).

Coastal defences

- In the UK this generally involves hard (structures built to resist wave energy) or soft (solutions that work with the environment and natural processes) engineering.

	Cliff face strategies	Cliff foot strategies	Beach management schemes
Hard engineering	Cliff pinning Cliff modification Drainage of cliffs Gabion baskets (Average costs £500 to £2000/m)	Sea walls (£1500 to £2000/m) Revetments (£300/m) Rip-Rap	Breakwaters (£120 000 each) Groynes (Wooden at £6000 each) Beach Pumping Reef Systems (£ millions)
	Over drying and subsistence. Gabions are useless as an erosion preventer.	Expensive to build and maintain. Walls cause accelerated erosion of the beach and allow beach levels to fall. Revetments have a short life cycle.	Groynes interrupt and reduce LSD as they are 100% efficient at trapping sand. They are visually intrusive. Reefs change beach plans and profiles.
Soft engineering	Revegetation	No engineering problems	Beach nourishment and replenishment (at a cost of £20/m³)
	Problems only relate to poor vegetation choice.	No problems	Nearshore dredged material can affect the sediment cell, impeding and disrupting replenishment. Recharged sediment needs to be of the same calibre as the natural sediment.

Planning and funding

- All Councils with responsibilities for coastal defences have strategies in place.
- *Shoreline Management Plans* (SMPs), are based on the so-called *Sediment Management Cells* (a way of dividing up the UK and Welsh coastline).
- These SMPs will identify the options available to the Coastal Managers and are known as *Management Units Options*
  Options include:
  - *Do nothing* – no action is taken to build or maintain defences.
  - *Hold the line* – interventional to hold defences where they are at present.
  - *Advance the line* – new measures introduced that move defences seaward.
  - *Managed retreat.*

Examiner's Tip

Note there is a strong relationship between the location of urban areas and thinly populated areas and the desire to protect the coast!

Coastal concerns

Coral reefs and atolls

- These are widespread between latitudes 30°N and 30°S in the western parts of the Pacific, Indian and Atlantic Oceans.
- They are either fringing, barrier or atollic in origin.
- They have a biological 'source', the remains of living and dead polyps, algae, foraminifera, molluscs and other shelly organisms in the presence of calcium carbonate contribute to the reef.
- Ideal sea conditions in which reefs form are where the salinity is in the order of 27 to 38 ppm, with a mean sea temperature of 18°C, and with an adequate circulation of sea water.
- Changing sea temperature distributions (attributed to El Niño) and global warming (causing SL changes) are affecting the continued development and growth of coral reefs.
- Destruction by human activity (tourism, over-fishing and wholesale destruction for export and pollution) and the crown-of-thorns sea star infestation has wrought destruction to vast areas.

Global warming

- This is the term given to increased temperatures on the Earth's surface, resulting from carbon dioxide and other gases trapping the incoming solar radiation.
- It results in the world's oceans increasing their volume (so called thermal expansion), a eustatic change.
- The predictions for future SL as a result of global warming for the next fifty to a hundred years are alarming, 80 million extra people will be flooded each year due to rising sea levels.
- Combined with an apparent increase in storminess, increased extreme tidal events and storm surges; lowland coastal areas will need enhanced protection from the sea.

Sea surges

- Seem to be an increasingly frequent phenomenon.
- They result from a number of concurrent, but freak conditions.
- In the North Sea they are caused by:
  - high tides
  - strong northerly winds (influenced by the presence of low pressure)
  - high pressure to the west of the North Sea and low pressure to the east
  - the bottleneck that is the southern North Sea and its lowland coast exacerbates the problem (as does global warming).
- Events this decade, in 1993, 1995 and 1999 caused flooding and damage to large parts of the Broads and coast of Norfolk and parts of coastal Western Europe.

Human impact on the oceans

- Increased awareness of the environment has led to added pressure to safeguard our natural coastline and has contributed to land-use conflict.
- The pollution of surface water and sub-surface water by chemicals released through industrial activities either directly into rivers or into the air, and by fertilisers used in agriculture, has led to pollution of coastal water.
- Nobody denies damage is being done, disagreement centres on the severity of damage.
- Our coastline must be conserved, protected and enhanced.

> **Examiner's Tip**
>
> Many of these concerns are regularly 'rehearsed' in the newspapers. Keep a number as case studies to use in the AS Level exam.

Progress check

1 Why do coasts usually exhibit a more equal balance of erosion and deposition than more inland sites?

2 How might wave refraction contribute to our understanding of the dynamic equilibrium of the coast?

3

Constructive wave	Features	Destructive wave
Low	Wave height	High
Low frequency (6 to 8/min)	Wave frequency	High frequency (13 to 15/min)
Low	Wave steepness	High

(a) Based on the above table how might energy on a beach be affected?

(b) Spits might result from the constructional activity of waves. What other factors contribute to spit formation? Where do they form?

4 Take one coastal landform feature. Explain how a combination of factors might form it.

5 Explain, with examples, why much of the coastal engineering around our coasts is controversial. What are the sustainable alternatives?

6 Outline one future coastal concern we may have to deal with in the future.

Answers on page 91

Population

Theories

- The growth of the world's population has dominated governments, planners and world history. In 1798 the Reverend Thomas Malthus wrote his *Essay on Population*, in which he warned that population would outstrip food supply.
- Paul Ehrlich also warned of impending disaster if the world's population was not brought under control; in *The Population Bomb*.

Global dynamics

Growth

- About a million or so years ago the first humans walked the earth.
- For thousands of years population changed little, probably reaching 25 0000 000 at the time of the Christian era.
- Change continued to remain low until the industrial revolution in Europe about 200 years ago.
- World population reached 1000 million in the early 19th century, 2000 million in the 1920s, 3000 million in the 1960s. An extra 1000 million added in 100, 40 and 10 years respectively.
- World population doubled between 1820 and 1920. It doubled again in 50 years up to the 70s. Theoretically it will double again in the next 30 years.
- The world's population is increasing at an increasing rate.
- World population in 2000 = 6 billion

The growth in world population

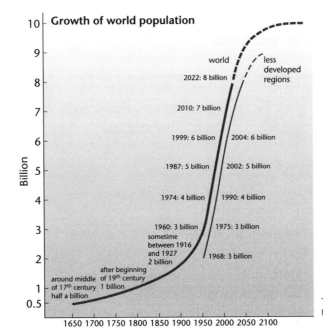

The state of the world population, UNFPA. UN Family Planning Association

Examiner's Tip

Population growth questions are common at AS Level because of the dynamic nature of the subject.

(Continued next page)

Global dynamics

Distribution

- Population has not increased evenly over the world.
- The growth rates of some North African Countries is in the order of 3% (enough to double the population in 25 years).
- Many European countries have experienced drops in population in recent years.
- It is estimated that 95% of world population growth will occur in Africa, Asia and Latin America over the next 25 years.

Measuring change

- *Natural increase* occurs when the number of births (birth rate = BR) exceeds the number of deaths (Death Rate = DR) in any one year.
- In addition, if the number of immigrants that join a country exceeds emigration, populations will rise.

    Fertility +/– Mortality +/– Migration = +/– Growth

- *Birth rate* is the number of live births/1000 people/year.
- *Crude death rate* (the number of deaths/1000 inhabitants/year) is the most common measure of mortality but its usefulness is limited, as it takes no account of population structure.
- *Infant mortality* (the number of deaths of infants under the age of one year old/1000 live births) is a better measure.

Reasons for change

- *Falling death rates* as a result of better medicines, improved sanitation, better diets.
- Through the 20th century Africa has seen death rates halved, particularly amongst children.
- The Northern Hemisphere generally has the lower DRs.
- *Birth rates* have fallen in MEDCs but not in LEDCs. As a result the populations of LEDCs will double over the next half-century while MEDCs populations will shrink.

Why birth rates decline in MEDCs

Reasons include:

- availability of family planning
- increased education and literacy
- better health and fewer child deaths
- more employment opportunities
- later marriage
- migration to the cities
- better deals for women
- more income and rising living standards.

Why LEDCs continue to have high BRs

The reasons for the continuing high BR in LEDCs are complex and include:

- the importance placed upon child-bearing in some countries
- large families are seen as insurance for the future
- women are dis-empowered
- more children = more workers.
- Generally population increase equates to high BRs (e.g. in Africa the BR is in excess of 40/1000; in Europe it's less than 15/1000!).

Examiner's Tip

It's important to understand all of this; it is good structured question and extended prose material!

Implications of increased population

If population increases the following will occur:

- there will be increased fuel consumption
- there will be increases in greenhouse effects, such as increased flooding, salinisation and rising sea levels
- increasing amounts of acid rain will strike the earth
- there will be a general increase in waste and pollution
- increased agricultural activity, equates to increases in pesticide and fertiliser use
- there will be an increased use, and therefore depletion, in the stocks of world minerals and hardwoods, etc.

The relationship between population and resources

	% of population	% resource consumption
MEDCs	25	80
LEDCs	75	20

Carrying capacity

- Carrying capacity is the ability of the earth to sustain human life. Resources can only be exploited to a certain level before they are exhausted.
- MEDC populations are stable but still consume a high proportion of global resources.
- As LEDCs drive to industrialise, their consumption will increase and so will pollution and environmental decay.
- The world can only sustain an inflated world population for a short time.

The concept of optimum population

- A measure of the ideal population to live and work in a given area. An optimum population is one that is in balance with the resources available and where GNP is optimised.
- *Over-population* occurs when population is > than resources.
- *Under-population* occurs when population is < than resources.

Under-population

Causes

- physical disadvantage, e.g. climate
- inaccessible/poor communications/remote
- historical, e.g. Australia
- types of economy, i.e. intensive manufacturing or agricultural with a small indigenous population, e.g. Brazil, 92% live in the SE, many natural resources are yet untouched; Canada, wealth is based on fish and forestry.

Consequences

- resources tend to be developed by foreign countries
- regional disparity is obvious
- high urbanisation
- high standard of living
- high immigration

N.B. Under-population does not imply a country is poor or has a low population density.

Examiner's Tip

The best AS Level students will provide accurate definitions of optimum, over- and under-population.

(Continued next page)

Global dynamics

Over-population

Opposing views

- *The Neo-Malthusian approach* – increasing population leads to environmental degradation, which limits population growth.
- *The Boserupian approach* (after Ester Boserup, a Danish Economist) – 'necessity is the mother of invention'. Increasing population drives agricultural productivity, which allows further increases in population.

Consequences

- starvation
- malnutrition
- poor health
- lack of jobs
- slow economic growth, e.g. India and Egypt

Population density and distribution

- *Density* A measure of the average number of people/unit area. This measure should not be used to compare countries in terms of over-population, as different countries have different carrying capacities.
- *Distribution* Relates to location based mainly on economic and physical factors. It is difficult to measure as it is a spatial indicator.

World population densities

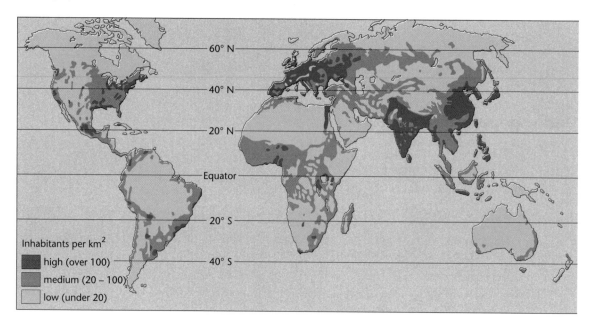

Examiner's Tip

Asking for a descriptive account of a data collection, map or diagram (like the one above) at AS Level is common, especially in structured questions.

The demographic transition model (DTM)

- *Crude Birth Rate* (CBR) and *Crude Death Rate* (CDR) can be used to analyse the change in the rate of natural increase over time and demographic transition.

The demographic transition model

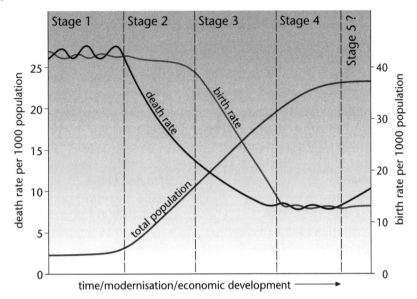

STAGE 1	STAGE 2	STAGE 3	STAGE 4
DR high – little medical care BR high – no birth control and children an economic advantage DR fluctuates due to plagues/famines	DR declines – medical developments and improved nutrition and sanitation BR remains high – children remain an economic advantage since urbanisation and mechanisation at an early stage, and births seen as desirable Increasing difference between BR and DR	DR low and slowly decreasing – continued medical and nutritional developments BR starts to decrease rapidly – improved education and availability of contraception and decreased economic value of children due to increasing urbanisation and use of technology Decreasing difference between BR and DR	DR remains low and slowly falling – continued medical progress and enhanced welfare provision BR declines to just above DR – economic independence of women, improved contraception and changing views on desirability of births in highly urbanised society
high proportion are young	very high proportion are young	increasing numbers surviving to old age	high proportion of population are ageing
Stage 1: high stationary *Pre-industrial society*	Stage 2: early expanding *Early industrialisation*	Stage 3: late expanding *Later industrialisation*	Stage 4: low stationary *Developed country*

Examiner's Tip

Adored by examiners. A favourite structured question and extended prose topic. You must know all there is to know on the DTM.

(Continued next page)

The demographic transition model (DTM)

Uses

DTM is used widely to predict future population patterns and numbers.

- Used as a descriptor, for comparison, for prediction, for explanation, as a starting point for discussion.
- It does not predict or assess when, or how long transitions will be.

Limitations

- Limited database.
- Migration is not assessed.
- External influences not considered.
- Does not go beyond stage 4 in the original model.
- It has variable validity, see below:

DTM and Europe

- Suggests fertility decline is even. European countries do vary.
- Suggests fertility decline be linked to increases in literacy, decreases in mortality and increased urbanisation.
- Ignores birth control in stage 1.
- Delays in child bearing ignored in later stages.
- Does the fertility of one generation determine the next?
- What effect pro-natalism, fascism and Catholicism?

DTM and LEDCs

- The transitions in mortality and fertility occur in a shorter time.
- Growth in population is greater in LEDCs.
- Comparisons with MEDCs, because of the above, are difficult.
- DRs have fallen faster, and for different reasons to Europe.
- Mass contraception availability has had an effect.

UK application

The fit of the DTM to the UK

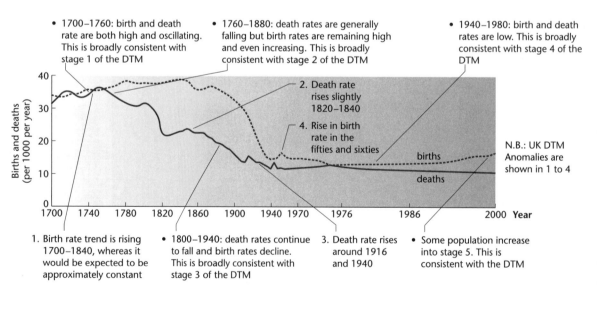

- 1700–1760: birth and death rate are both high and oscillating. This is broadly consistent with stage 1 of the DTM

- 1760–1880: death rates are generally falling but birth rates are remaining high and even increasing. This is broadly consistent with stage 2 of the DTM

- 1940–1980: birth and death rates are low. This is broadly consistent with stage 4 of the DTM

2. Death rate rises slightly 1820–1840

4. Rise in birth rate in the fifties and sixties

N.B.: UK DTM Anomalies are shown in 1 to 4

births

deaths

1. Birth rate trend is rising 1700–1840, whereas it would be expected to be approximately constant

- 1800–1940: death rates continue to fall and birth rates decline. This is broadly consistent with stage 3 of the DTM

3. Death rate rises around 1916 and 1940

- Some population increase into stage 5. This is consistent with the DTM

Examiner's Tip

Knowing and understanding this additional DTM information will put you in a league ahead of the rest!

Why did mortality decline?

- Improved sanitation and hygiene.
- Improved food supply.
- Reduction in disease impact.
- Medical advances.
- Rise in living standard.

Why did fertility decline?

- Legislation to do with female and child labour.
- More women in the work force.
- Contraception.
- Declining infant mortality.

LEDC applications

Most are bunched in the second stage, unable to achieve economic and social progress to enable them to move on. Population increases and ecological problems further hamper progress. However, there have been notable decreases in mortality and fertility in the last 100 years.

Why has mortality decreased?

- Malaria and other tropical bugs have been eradicated or controlled.
- Improved health care.
- Stronger economies.
- Better nutrition.

Why has fertility decreased?

- Age of marriage has increased.
- Contraception.
- Urbanisation/Western values have been taken on.
- The status of women has improved.

Population structure

Population pyramids

- Population pyramids are a graphical method of representing the age and sex structure of a population at one point in time.
- The shape of a country's pyramid reflects demographic and socio-economic changes; past fertility, mortality and migration, the incidence of 'baby booms', wars, epidemics, population planning policies, etc.
- On the pyramid data is expressed in percentages facilitating comparison of age–sex ratios between countries.

Three main types

(a) stationary

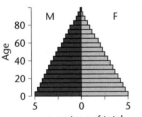

(b) progressive

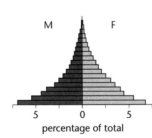

(c) regressive

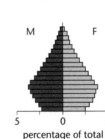

(d) composite

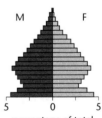

Stationary

Population unchanged over a long period of time.
Is regular and tapering, e.g. Equador.

Progressive

BR is increasing
DR is still high, e.g. Bangladesh.

Regressive

Decline in BR, lower mortality. 'Bell-shaped' pattern, e.g. Japan.

Composite

Attributes of two or more, of 1 and 2.

Examiner's Tip

Learn the above pyramid shapes and be able to apply them to a range of LEDCs and MEDCs.

(Continued next page)

Population structure

Dependency

The Dependency Ratio

- This is one of the most common measures derived from population pyramids.
- For convenience the age structure is divided into three broad age bands:
  - youthful dependants aged 1 to 14
  - elderly dependants aged 65 and over
  - working population aged 15 to 64.
- To calculate the proportions of dependants is simple. The proportions of young and old are divided by the proportion who are economically active, to yield a ratio.
- If the dependant group constitutes a relatively high proportion, the ratio will be high.
- The greater the proportion in the working age group the fewer the dependants.
- Dependency ratios are higher for developing countries.

Points to bear in mind

- Is a young dependant more of a burden on a working person's resources than an elderly dependant?
- Many over 15s continue to study so this age group is now incorrectly classified in the working population.
- In many LEDCs children start jobs at young ages.
- How should students, housewives and the unemployed be classified?

Trends in population structure

LEDCs

- BR is still high, but reducing.
- The numbers of those who are 15 or less is still very high.
- There are more old people.
- Population will continue to increase; anti-natal population policies will be imposed to deal with increased population.
- Pressure increases on the countries' economies.
- Children need to work.
- Migration increases.
- Unrest and instability within the country.

MEDCs

- Increased numbers of elderly.
- The upper end of the population structure is increasingly fit and healthy.
- Reduced BRs.
- Decline in the working population.
- Tax burden on workers increases.
- Greater Government spending.
- Fit OAPs retire later: career paths for younger people close because of this.
- The state is unable to fully provide for OAPs.
- The elderly are moneyed and mobile.
- Growth in 'grey' investment/economy.
- Holidays and retirement homes increase.

The 'greying' world population

- As countries become 'developed' they experience a static population with low BRs and DRs.
- The lowering of the DR is seen by many as the population explosion of the 21st century.
- By 2050 1:7 of the world's population will be over 60.

Consequences

- *Supporting the elderly* In MEDCs, the old will have to finance their retirement, with fewer people working there is not the revenue to support the State Pension System.
- *Impact on young* Fewer children mean fewer babies, which means fewer workers and leads to unstable structures and economies.

Examiner's Tip

Dependency is a current problem and therefore important at AS Level!

Migration

Technology and economic progress influence mobility. Increased mobility makes increased migration possible. Migration is usually defined as a 'change of residence of substantial duration'.

Classification

Migration can be classified by:

Time-scale
- seasonal in nature, e.g. Mexican fruit pickers in California
- temporary, e.g. asylum seekers
- periodic, e.g. forced out by conflict
- permanent (over 1+ years), e.g. emigration to New Zealand.

Distance
- internal – within cities
- external – a move abroad
- inter-regional – a job move
- international – emigration/immigration.

Causation
- forced, e.g. Kosovan refugees
- spontaneous
- free, could be politically, socially or economically motivated
- planned.

Traits of migrants

Age
- The majority of migrants are aged between 18 and 35, often moving for a first job.
- The young adjust more easily to different environments.
- Increasingly people migrate on retirement.

Sex
- In general in MEDCs male and females migrate in roughly equal amounts.
- In LEDCs it tends to be the young males.

Marital status
- In advanced countries most migrants have in the past been single.
- Nowadays family migrations are more common.

Occupational groups
- Professional migrants tend to predominate.
- Occupational migrations tend to be selective in terms of race, nationality and education.

Examiner's Tip

Continually in the news. Keep your scrapbook up to date! Good case studies appear just about every day.

(Continued next page)

Migration

Causes

Migration stimulating conditions include:

- marriage
- lack of wedlock
- employment offers
- increased mechanisation in agriculture
- the migrant has special skills
- low wages at origin
- retirement
- highly political, racial or oppressive governments at origin
- natural disasters
- forced migration.

'Push' and 'pull' factors both cause migration

- 'Push' factors occur at the place of origin.
- 'Pull' factors occur at the destination.

Factors in the choice of destination include:

- cost of moving
- presence of friends and relatives
- employment
- amenities
- features of the physical environment
- assistance and subsides
- information available
- lack of alternative destinations.

Socio-economic factors influencing migration include:

- technological change
- changes in economic practice and organisation
- propaganda
- regulations on migration
- healthcare and education
- population pressure
- climate and vegetation
- natural barriers
- size of countries.

Migration models

These attempt to summarise our understanding of migration into a series of typologies. Most models look at:

- the distance travelled by a migrant
- internal and international movement
- the permanence of migration
- the causes of migration and its selectivity.

Examiner's Tip

Push and pull factors. Learn them! They complete your understanding of migration.

Peterson's Typology of Migration

- He identified five classes of migration: primitive, forced, impelled, free and mass movements.
- Each was seen to have an activating force, and initiator.
- Each class of migration is then further sub-divided into conservative migrants and innovating migrants.

Zelinsky's Mobility Transition Model

- This is a five-phase model.
- In phase one there is just cyclic movement.
- In phase two massive movement occurs.
- By stage four migration has levelled off.
- By phase five the only real movements are temporary inter-urban movements.
- Zelinsky's model closely mirrors the DTM and certainly seems to fit the patterns of migration seen in the developed world.
- Zelinsky argued that migration is on the whole an orderly event.

Lee's Laws of Migration

- Outlines why groups choose to migrate.
- Summarises the ideas of 'push and pull' models.
  - There are factors linked to the destination of the migrants.
  - There are factors associated with the origins of the migrants.
  - Some intervening obstacles exist between origin and destination.
  - Personal factors come into play.

Ravenstein's Laws of Migration

These were developed on the basis of migration for Great Britain between 1871 and 1881.

- He outlined eleven laws as follows:
  - The majority of migrants go only a short distance.
  - Migration proceeds step by step.
  - Migrants going long distances generally go by preference to one of the great centres of commerce or industry.
  - Each current of migration produces a compensating counter-current.
  - The natives of towns are less migratory than those of rural areas.
  - Females are more migratory than males within the kingdom of their birth, but males more frequently venture beyond.
  - Most migrants are adults; families rarely migrate out of their country of birth.
  - Large towns grow more by migration than by natural increase.
  - Migration increases in volume as industries and commerce develop and transport improves.
  - The major direction of migration is from the agricultural areas to the centres of industry and commerce.
  - The major causes of migration are economic.

Examiner's Tip

All these models have a part to play in understanding how and why people migrate, take a little from all of them and learn thoroughly what you read.

(Continued next page)

Migration

Types of migration

Internal

- Migrants move from areas of perceived deprivation to areas of perceived promise.
- Various criteria are assigned to internal movements in an attempt to classify them.
- Causes of movement tend to be either compulsory or voluntary.
- They can also be temporary (like the cyclic movements of commuters in and out of a city) or permanent.
- Rural to urban is the dominant internal migration process.
- A push component drives people away from the rural areas.
- A pull component, 'the so-called bright light syndrome' attracts migrants to the cities.

International

- Economic motives are most important in international migration.
- In general, a nation receives migrants from countries less developed than it.
- Migrants tend to be either young and unskilled males or females or highly skilled professionals.
- An alternative name for this type of movement is work or wage-related migration.
- An example is the *Gastarbeiter* from Turkey that moved to Germany after the war.

Refugees

- A refugee is a person moved outside their own country because they are being persecuted because of their race, political or religious belief.
- If granted refugee status they become asylum seekers.
- There are in excess of 20 000 000 refugees in the world.
- The burden of housing these people is borne, on the whole, by the developing countries of the world.
- The Western approach is to tighten restrictions on migration.
- An example are Kosovars forced out of Kosovo by the Serbs.

Who gains from migration?

Country of emigration

Gains include:
- less unemployment
- money sent back helps raise living standards
- migrants may return and bring back new skills to help development.

Losses include:
- most able and ambitious leave: they are best able to help development of their own country
- family stress if split up for length of time
- unemployment raised if returning migrants cannot find work.

Country of immigration

Gains include:
- jobs done cheaply
- willing workforce to train
- allows country to develop further
- overcomes short-term labour shortage and such workers are easy to dispose of during periods of recession.

Losses include:
- money sent out of country
- immigrants may not integrate: tensions build up with native people
- problems of immigrants in times of high unemployment.

Examiner's Tip

There are winners and losers in migration. Ensure you can deliver both sides of the story! Know plenty of case studies.

Population control

- Population projections often spur governments to establish policies.
- Policies influence growth, mortality, fertility, distribution and migration.

Anti-natalist policies

- Methods include:
  - providing contraception advice and devices/pills
  - legalised abortion and late marriages
  - economic and social measures to discourage large families.

India

- At the end of the last century India's population was about 1 billion.
- Population growth was supported by agricultural advances and improvements in health.
- Recognising that growth couldn't continue indefinitely the country adopted an ambitious programme of family planning and welfare.
- This was initially based on sterilisation – forced in some cases.
- It was soon realised it was better to educate women to prefer smaller, healthier families.
- The programme is now much more about advice than action

Kenya

- The Kenya Government refused to impose or even suggest an ideal family size. Inheritance laws exclude female offspring so families continue to try for boys if initial births are female!
- The high proportion of Catholics further hinders birth control.
- Recently the Kenyan government pledged to reduce population growth by the next census. We wait and see!

China's 'one-child policy'

- 'Every stomach comes with a pair of hands' according to Maoist philosophy.
- Mao's worst mistake was to encourage population growth in an attempt to boost the Chinese economy.
- China's ever-growing population has negated all the economic gains made since 1940.
- The ruthless one-child policy was introduced in 1979.
- It carried financial penalties and prison sentences for those that dared deviate from it. In the early 1990s the Chinese realised things were going wrong.
  - Rules were lax in the countryside.
  - Female infanticide and abortions quadrupled.
  - The rural population was still growing and outgrowing educational provision.
  - A single-child policy cannot support a massive greying population.
- Intellectuals now feel that China was mistaken in both its policy to encourage population growth and its policy to control it!

Pro-natalist policies

- These encourage population growth.
- They were established where governments believe that strength in numbers will lead to economic prosperity.
- Examples include:
  - France with its 'La famille est prioritaire' scheme.
  - The Romanian scheme under the rule of President Ceausescu.
  - Malaysian and German schemes offering maternity benefits and tax concessions to families that enlarge.

Examiner's Tip

It is obviously wise to know some population policies. But ensure you know which have been successful and which have failed.

Progress check

1 Write single-sentence definitions for each of the following words and phrases. Remember to learn your answers.

- population change
- crude death rate
- natural increase
- age/sex pyramids
- distribution of population
- immigration
- dependency
- birth rate
- push v pull
- infant mortality

2 (a) What was Malthus' understanding of the relationship between population and resources?

(b) Outline ideas and theories that have replaced those of Malthus.

3 Outline some of the reasons why population has grown so rapidly in the last 50 years in LEDCs.

4 Why is it that optimum populations are rarely attained?

5 What are the social and economic consequences for MEDCs of an increasing number of people over 65 years of age?

6 Three types of population policy exist: namely anti-natalist policies, transmigration and immigration control. Outline very briefly how each policy operates, and offer some examples to support your answers.

7 Refer to the population pyramids on page 59 to help you draw actual pyramids for countries you select. Label your examples and describe the main features of the pyramids you have drawn.

8 Evaluate the usefulness and limitations of the demographic transition model. (This is a common question at AS Level.)

Answers on page 91–92

Settlement

- Settlements are usually defined as 'a place in which people live and where they may be involved in various activities'.

Early settlement

- Before settling in an area, early farmers would have studied a range of factors.
- Factors include availability of clean water, freedom from flooding, level land for building and farming, timber for fuel and building, cultivable and grazeable soils, trade and commercial possibilities and defence.
- **Site** refers to the area upon which a settlement is built.
- **Situation** refers to the relative location of a settlement to other features.

Rural/urban characteristics

- Various ways have been formulated to distinguish between rural and urban settlements in the UK.
- Many of these characteristics apply equally well to other MEDCs and to LEDCs but variations between countries can be marked.

Rural settlement (villages, hamlets and farms)

- Employment mostly in agriculture.
- Social homogeneity, interaction and involvement.
- Age structure: lots of 5 to 24 year olds and over 65s.
- A small number of functions (i.e. a general store, sub post office and a pub).
- Low density of population.
- Dispersed settlement.
- Poorly developed infrastructure.
- Census classifies it as rural.
- There is land, as opposed to real money.
- Religion is important.
- Inhabitants have a common purpose and community is generally inward looking.
- Rural areas can be open, closed, disintegrated or integrated.

Urban settlement (cities and towns)

- Employment is mostly in commerce, services and manufacturing.
- Socially heterogeneous.
- Ages 24 to 54 predominate.
- There is a wide range (maybe hundreds) of functions (e.g. department store, banks, hospitals, etc.).
- High-density of population.
- High-density, closely packed housing.
- Biggest proportion of the population was born outside the urban centre.
- Limited responsibilities towards neighbours.
- Well-developed infrastructure.
- The census classifies the area as urban.
- Length of residence tends to be short.
- 'No' religion.

Examiner's Tip

Comparisons of urban and rural areas is common at this level. Though the AS specifications all have a bias towards urban rather than rural geography.

Hierarchy

- Settlements offer a range of services – or **functions**.
- Services provide for the people who live in a settlement and those within travelling distance.

A hierarchy graph to show how the number of functions vary with population size.

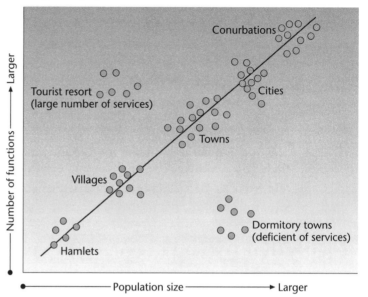

Settlement models

Christalle: Central place theory (1933)

Use To explain the size and spacing of settlements in MEDCs.

Assumptions That people who live in hamlets obtain low order goods locally, visiting high order settlements to obtain goods not locally available. It's expected that high order settlements will be a minimal distance away. A hierarchy starts to reveal itself.

Results There appears to be a maximum distance people will travel for goods (range). There is a minimum number of people needed to keep a service in place (threshold). Every settlement has a sphere of influence (the area it serves). The above is described as Christaller's K=3 principle.

Advantages and disadvantages It has been used in rural planning, is comparative and on the flat plain it is designed for, works! Problems arise because people are not rational. Theory deals only with goods and services and chance plays a part in settlement location and pattern.

Central places

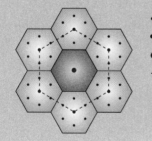

- • villages
- • town
- • city
- - - - sphere of influence

Losch: City rich and city poor (1941)

Use To explain the patterns of settlement in MEDCs

Assumptions That all settlements of the same size don't have the same functions. Sizes of central places vary with distance. Distinctive city rich: city poor pattern of sectors emerges.

Results Losch's theory appears to fit many of today's distributions, e.g. city poor equates to Aldershot and city rich to the Thames corridor, north of Aldershot, and the Reigate and Guildford areas to the south of Aldershot.

Advantages and disadvantages It is complex but does fit today's distributions.

Taafe, Morrill and Gould: Transport model (1970)

Uses Transport networks are used to develop and explain settlement patterns and emergence.

Assumptions That ports are built and penetrate into the hinterland, nodes or smaller settlements develop and grow on the intersections and routeways out of the port.

Advantages and disadvantages It is dynamic, functional and explanatory.

Examiner's Tip

Models are used a lot in AS Level questions on the rural/urban world. Know the terminology.

Morphology

Rural patterns

Nucleated Houses and buildings are clustered. Traditional in the UK because of the enclosure system, defence and the need for water, e.g. Urchfont, Wiltshire.

Dispersed Farms and buildings widely scattered. Common in sparsely populated areas, e.g. Oby, Norfolk.

Linear Spread along a trade or transport route, e.g. Sutton Row, Norfolk.

Cruciform Settlement occurs at the intersection of roads, e.g. Potterne, Wiltshire.

Green Village A cluster of dwellings around a village green, e.g. Kimberley and Old Buckenham in Norfolk.

Urban land use models: MEDCs

These describe city layouts and are very simple.

'Bid rent theory' – that the value of land decreases away from the most central areas – underlies many of these models.

Burgess: Concentric model (1920)

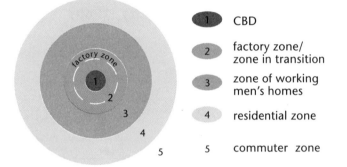

1   CBD

2   factory zone/zone in transition

3   zone of working men's homes

4   residential zone

5   commuter zone

- City grows because of immigration and natural increase.
- Social class increases with distance from the CBD.
- CBD is dominated by commercial activity.
- Population density peaks in the high density, low cost housing zone.

Hoyt: Sector model (1939)

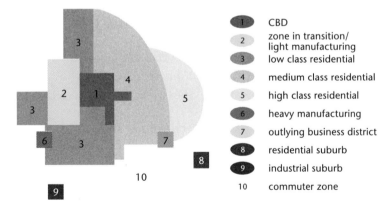

1   CBD

2   zone in transition/light manufacturing

3   low class residential

4   medium class residential

5   high class residential

6   heavy manufacturing

7   outlying business district

8   residential suburb

9   industrial suburb

10   commuter zone

- Emphasised that cities don't have a single centre.
- Cities grow and envelop other centres.
- New industrial sites arise.

> **Examiner's Tip**
>
> Cities are dynamic and unique, they are studied extensively at AS Level.

(Continued next page)

Morphology

Harris and Ullman: Multiple nuclei model (1945)

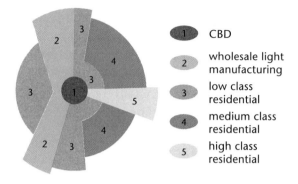

1. CBD
2. wholesale light manufacturing
3. low class residential
4. medium class residential
5. high class residential

- Hoyt emphasised the role of transport related to sector development.
- He thought that certain activities deterred others.
- Better housing is away from industry.

Mann: Model land use in the UK city (1960)

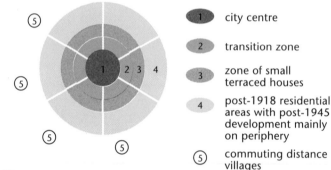

1. city centre
2. transition zone
3. zone of small terraced houses
4. post-1918 residential areas with post-1945 development mainly on periphery
5. commuting distance villages

- East/west split.
- East = working class and industry.
- West = clean and wealthy people's homes.

Urban land models: LEDCs (Latin America)

- Many cities have grown haphazardly and are a jumble of different activities and buildings without a clear structure.
- Large areas may be dedicated to residential land use without any commercial centres.
- Industries may be located in central urban areas.
- Airports may be within sprawling cities as expansion exceeds capacity to build infrastructures.
- High-class housing with excellent services may be next to shanty towns lacking even the most basic amenities.

When looking at models of urban growth in LEDCs you should always reflect that:

- Urbanisation and in-migration occurs on an immense scale.
- Urban planning and financial support is negligible.
- The driving force for expansion is residential growth, with administrative, commercial and industrial coming a poor second.

Griffin and Ford: Latin American concentric ring model

- Concentric model (similar to Burgess), with the oldest area in the centre – the old Colonial City.
- The growth of the cities occurred late in the last century and was largely unplanned.
- As most migrants could not afford to buy homes they engaged in self-build housing, e.g. *callampas* in Santiago de Chile, or *favelas* in Rio de Janeiro.

- Settlement usually achieved by illegal occupation of land on the urban periphery or on unsuitable sites in the city centre, e.g. steep hills like the *morros* in Rio, riverbanks/flood plains like Rio Bogota in Bogota; or building sites.
- Slowly shanty dwellings improved and became part of the city. Houses were rebuilt with more permanent materials, and roads and utilities provided.
- New areas of temporary accommodation developed further out from the centre and the process began again.
- Little allowance was made for industry, recreation or commercial land uses.
- This model applies to cities whose growth is unconfined physically, e.g. Mexico City, Mexico, developed on dried up lakebeds.

The concentric ring model of urban growth

The concentric ring model of urban growth   **Sectoral model of urban growth**

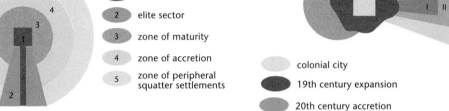

1	CBD and extensions
2	elite sector
3	zone of maturity
4	zone of accretion
5	zone of peripheral squatter settlements

colonial city

19th century expansion

20th century accretion

elite sector expansion I, II, III

Sectoral model of urban growth

- This is a different kind of model.
- It relies on less rapid growth and strong physical restraints such as mountain topography.
- It applies to Andean cities along the Pacific Coast. Others include: Caracas, Venezuela; sited in a narrow E–W valley with steep slopes prohibiting development.
- Growth is linear rather than concentric.
- The outer expansion is not due to shantytown growth but to movement of the élite, occupying large areas at a low density.
- The poor serve to fill up rather than form the growth on the edge of the city.

Urbanisation and urban growth

- In 1900 about 2% of population lived in urban areas.
- In 2000 50%+ (nearly 3 billion people) live in urban areas, though clearly this percentage varies across the globe.
- In the past agricultural surpluses caused urban growth and development.
- Today movement to the city is seen as a change in location, and lifestyles, as people are absorbed into a global society and economy.
- Reasons for urbanisation are similar in both MEDCs and LEDCs.
- Three processes are involved: urban growth, spreading urbanism, and urbanisation.

Urban growth

- This refers to the growth in size of urban centres due to population increases.
- World urban growth correlates with world population growth.
- Most of this growth is occurring in the LEDCs; most MEDCs have static urban growth.
- LEDCs experiencing rapid urban growth still have large numbers of rural dwellers.

Examiner's Tip

Settlement questions at AS Level tend to be thematic, focusing on a limited number of topics.

(Continued next page)

Urbanisation and urban growth

Spreading urbanism

- Refers to the social and behavioural characteristics of those living an urban existence, the fostering of shared activities and tastes.
- Urbanism or urban 'culture' has changed completely the views of many Europeans and Americans.
- Most African and Asian city-dwellers have yet to taste this 'culture'.

Urbanisation

- Refers to increases in the proportions of those living in towns and cities.
- Involves a shift of populations from rural to urban locations.
- In both LEDCs and MEDCs urbanisation is seen as a cyclic process.
- Populations move from rural to industrial economies until a balance of about 3:1/urban : rural is reached when growth flattens out.
- When urbanisation has run its course, as in MEDCs, people return to the countryside.
- Urbanisation is quickest in Asia and Africa at the moment.

Global pressures to urbanise

- It is generally agreed that urban growth and urbanisation over the last half century have been driven by the burgeoning global economy.
- Cities have developed as command centres for national, regional (and in some cases global) management of finance.
- In Asia the global economy has almost single handedly caused urban development.
- Transnational/multinational companies have concentrated their factory production in countries and locations (i.e. near ports for export reasons) with a cheap and available labour pool and a growing home market for products.
- Such industrial provision makes the city look even more attractive than usual for the rural poor!

The British experience

- At the beginning of the 18th century Britain was largely a rural farming economy. The largest city was London, other cities and towns, like Bristol and Norwich acted as market centres for agricultural products.
- Agricultural intensification leading to greater food production, drove many off the land and into the cities in search of work.
- The percentage living in rural areas in 1801 was about 35%, by 1901 it had risen to 78%.
- The 19th century was a period of rapid industrialisation.
- Industry was located in the towns and cities and new job opportunities and higher wages attracted thousands to move to cities.
- Rapid rural to urban migration occurred: the young, innovative and energetic moved to cities.
- By 1901 there were 33 cities of 100 000+, in 1801 there had been only one, London!
- Cities in Victorian Britain became noisy, dirty, congested and dangerous places, packed with factories and plagued by disease.
- People who could afford to, moved to the suburbs (suburbanisation) away from the filth and squalor.

Examiner's Tip

Remember that cities expand in phases and that many of the original uses became 'fossilised' within the new urban fabric.

- Aided by the development of the tram and railway networks the larger towns and cities of the UK began to spread beyond their original boundaries.

How urban areas developed

- Through *isolation*, for effective government in the towns and boroughs of the UK.
- Through *interaction*, roads and rail bringing trade and people closer together.
- Through the *growth of conurbations*, with industrialisation transforming towns and cities.
- Through the *growth of an axial belt*, stretching between Merseyside, through the Midlands to London and the SE.
- *The metropolis develops*, with the continued growth of London and the SE.

The Latin American experience

- City areas are not new to the continent; many date back to the time of the Aztecs and Incas.
- Most were initially established as ports during the colonial rule of European countries, for export, administration and commercial purposes.
- Most of the biggest urban areas are on Latin America's coast; on the whole few people live in the interior.
- In the last 50 years the urban population of Latin America has risen exponentially: it has quite literally exploded.
- Latin America was nearly totally rural in make up, now over 50% live in urban areas.
- The size, speed and scale of urbanisation has been massive on this continent.
- The biggest period of urban growth has been over the last 50 or 60 years, with growth rates between 5% and 2%.
- In most Latin American countries one city still dominates; though the single dominant primate city is becoming a thing of the past.
- Many of the middle-rank cities are taking on the roles of government, both political and financial, as they continue to grow.
- Latin American like European cities grow as a result of migration and natural increase but the growth has been compressed into a much smaller time frame.

Mega-cities

- Definition: a city with a population exceeding 8 000 000.
- In 1950 there were just two, London and New York. Today there are at least 25, 19 of them in LEDCs.

Factors influencing mega-city growth

- Rural to urban migration.
- Former ports, continue to develop as trading sites.
- Industrialisation related to international production continue in huge (often trans-national, foreign owned) sites.
- Industrial technology transfer also attracts people.
- Decreasing death rates due to better medical provision result in natural population increases.
- National development policies encourage or force people into the urban areas.
- Most mega-cities have slower growth now, than the millionaire cities (those with populations between 1 and 8 million).
- Both MEDCs and LEDCs now have to discover how to manage these sprawling settlements.

Examiner's Tip

The rapid change and growth of cities in LEDCs make this a popular examination question.

(Continued next page)

Urbanisation and urban growth

Problems and advantages

Problems

- Mega-cities become magnets for immigration.
- Shanty town and squatter settlements spontaneously appear.
- Hospitals and universities are located in the wealthier urban areas; rural areas have little or no provision.
- Informal employment grows but contributes little to the national economy.
- Poor air quality.
- A lack of clean/potable water
- Health problems associated with the above, i.e. asthma and cholera.
- Habitat loss.
- Crime and violence.
- Drug-related problems.
- Planning and administration are not co-ordinated.

Advantages

- Concentration of industry and the finance ensures economies of scale.
- General education and services are better in the big urban areas than they are in rural areas.
- Migrants deal with the housing problem in LEDCs!
- As you can see, the problems far outweigh the advantages.

Primacy and the rank size rule

- The rank size rule was first drawn up in the 1940s, by Zipf.
- He discovered an inverse relationship between the size and rank of a given settlement, i.e. the population of the second city in a country will be about half that of the biggest.
- This suggests that in any country there will be a few large places and many small ones.
- We can say that a country has high primacy if it exceeds the rank size rule prediction and low primacy if it is less than the prediction.
- Primacy is linked to development.
- Rank size patterns appear in countries that are smaller than average, have only recently urbanised or have simple economic and social structures.
- The rank-size rule does not explain settlement distributions, but does help to establish relationships between the size and importance of towns and cities.

Urban problems

Big cities have always suffered from overcrowding, crime, psychological stress, traffic chaos and pollution whether in a LEDC or MEDC. A problem from each is explored in a little more detail:

LEDC's – shanty towns

- There are in excess of 250 000 000 people living in the shanty towns of the LEDCs.
- Shanty towns exist because the authorities just cannot keep pace with the influx of migrants to the city.

Characteristics

- Unable to live in permanent housing people are forced to live in spontaneous settlements that they have built themselves, that use cheap waste materials, lack services (electricity, running water and rubbish collection), and are often sited in dangerous and vulnerable positions.
- They are overcrowded and harbour criminals.

- These conditions result in massive health problems, mostly related to dirty water, but compounded by poor diet. The shanty dwellers are the urban poor, the old rural poor, nothing changes for them.
- The young and better-educated are the migrants that 'make it' in the growing LEDC city.
- There are a range of problems that the authorities have to attend to avoid shanty towns spreading uncontrollably and blighting the city.

Problems

- Visual ugliness; they are an eyesore.
- High incidence of disease and health problems in a large population.
- Fire hazard.
- Site hazards, most are on vulnerable sites, i.e. steep slopes, land that is regularly flooded or likely to collapse when earthquakes strike.
- Organised street crime and the drug trade use them as a base for trading and a convenient repository of goods.
- House prices in nearby areas are severely depressed.

Solutions

- Some solutions are very destructive, e.g. bulldozing which happens periodically around the world.
- It is better to recognise that shanties serve a useful function.
- Make land available for new arrivals to the city.
- Make some tenure available, perhaps a ten-year lease.
- Make cheap material and waste materials available for building purposes.
- Introducing advisors into the 'towns' to help with construction advice.
- Encourage a sense of community.
- Lay the pads for 'self help' housing, and provide basic services, for new arrivals to build on.
- Invest in rural areas to stem flow from the countryside.

MEDC's – The UK's suburban sprawl

- By the end of the First World War London's urban area extended some 11 km from the centre, enabled by the growth of the railway.
- Most suburbs are the remnants of the villages that surrounded the city.
- The advent of the car accelerated the process, as did the relocation of industry to the suburbs.
- The imposition of green belt status has slowed the process but London is effectively surrounded by a suburban doughnut. Today London suburbs stretching some 80+ km from the centre in places.
- Similar processes happen around all cities, in Norwich urban growth has swallowed up many of the suburban villages around the city, i.e. Catton, Eaton, Cringleford and Thorpe.

Characteristics of suburbs	Advantages of suburbs	Disadvantages of suburbs
• linear in nature • low density, low storey housing, with gardens and owner occupied • middle income families • cul de sac /crescent and avenue layouts • near modes of mass transport	• cheaper land prices • modern houses with amenities • pleasant /clean pollution-free environment • better schools? • parks and gardens • less crime	• increasing cost of housing • lack of things to do in predominantly residential areas • young people prefer the city, this changes the population structure • difficulty of travel to the city: congestion and cost

Examiner's Tip

How change affects the suburbs (and inner city) is a favourite at AS Level.

(Continued next page)

Urban problems

Counterurbanisation

- A movement away from the city and into smaller more community-based towns.
- Evident during the 70s and early 80s in Europe and the USA.
- Reasons for this include:
  - retiree's moving to a more pleasant environment
  - new towns growing outside the city attracting workers
  - decentralisation, due to high city rents
  - the flight of city dwellers away from the congestion, stress and pollution of the city.
- Urbanisation is now seen to pass through five important stages or phases:
  1. people migrate from the countryside to the city
  2. the pace of migration accelerates, suburbs grow
  3. inner cities lose their populations
  4. the whole city region loses population due to counterurbanisation
  5. the population stabilises and people begin to return to the city: reurbanisation.

UK city centres

- The Central Business District (CBD) is generally at the heart of the city and is the focus of transport systems.
- The great accessibility of the CBD means that land is very expensive and limited in availability.
- CBDs display many common characteristics.

Main features of central business districts

Concentration of shops	Concentration of offices	Little manufacturing industry	Growth of functional zones	Multi-storey development	Low residential population
Large department stores, such as Marks and Spencer, C&A, and British Home Stores, are found at the heart of CBD. They attract large numbers of people from a wide area. Other specialist shops, such as book shops and jewellers, are also concentrated in the CBD.	Regional and head offices of large companies concentrate in the CBD. They are attracted by the accessibility of the city centre. Well-known companies like a well-known location for their head offices.	The CDB is not a suitable location for most manufacturing industries. However, a few specialised industries, such as newspaper and magazine publishers, do locate in the CBD. They need to be near to other CBD services and to have access to road and rail transport for distribution.	Similar activities tend to concentrate in certain parts of the CBD. It is usually possible to find areas given over almost entirely to entertainment, banks and financial services, educational facilities and shops.	The CBD has to grow upwards as well as outwards because of high land values. The most expensive sites have the tallest buildings. In a multi-storey block different activities may often occupy different floors.	There is little housing in the CBD because of the high land values. However, a few people live in luxury flats and apartments.

Source: Urban Landscapes, MacDonald Edre

Core-frame model

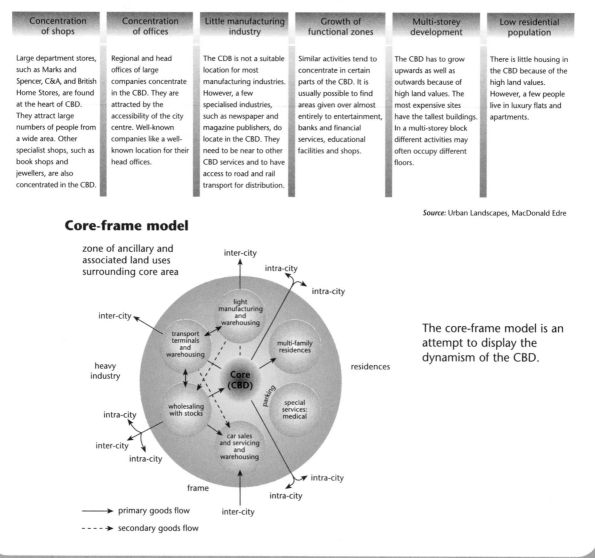

The core-frame model is an attempt to display the dynamism of the CBD.

- Large cities often have recognisable land-use areas, i.e. financial areas, department store areas and other specialist areas.
- The CBD changes constantly and continually to keep pace with a changing society.
- The *Core-Frame Model* attempts to reflect some of this dynamism. There are strong links between the core and frame; with areas/businesses constantly being assimilated and discarded from the core and frame.
- Elements of redevelopment, decentralisation, pedestrianisation, conservation and gentrification further complicate the pattern in the CBD.

The changing pattern of urban functions
- In the days before the car, shopping needs were satisfied locally on the street corner or on the high street. Things have changed, see below.
- Increasingly location reflects a community's population, wealth and the infrastructure of the area.
- Spiralling town/city centre rents have forced offices out of the centre and into a range of cheaper and more advantageous sites around the city.
- Suburbanisation has contributed to these changes, see below.

office locations

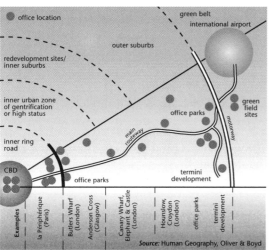

Source: Human Geography, Oliver & Boyd

retail locations

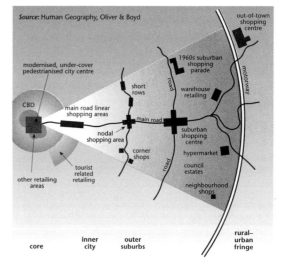

Beyond the CBD – the inner city
The festering problems of the 4 000 000 that live in the inner city areas of the UK came to a head about twenty years ago.

- There were a number of serious riots, urban unrest and increased crime and racial attacks.
- This happened despite half a century of major government policy initiatives directed at inner city problems.
- In 1947 *Comprehensive Development Areas Policy* spawned the *New and Expanded Towns Act*
- *General Improvement and Urban Programme* policies were formulated in the 60s.
- *Community Programmes and Development Projects* were set up in the early 70s.
- The *Urban Areas Act* of the late 70s led to *Action for Cities* and the formation of *Urban Development Corporations*, *City Action Teams* and the *Inner City Initiatives* in the late 80s.
- It was not, however, until the late 80s that the problems caused by lack of decent housing, jobs and recreation facilities began to be dealt with.

Examiner's Tip

The best AS candidates are able to apply their knowledge of CBD theory to chosen examples and case studies.

It's vital you know and understand the reasons for suburbanisation, i.e. social, planning, economic and commercial reasons.

(Continued next page)

Urban problems

- The range of problems that had to dealt with in the inner city are displayed below:

Environmental problems
- pollution
- vandalism
- dereliction
- lack of open space
- decaying housing
- poorly built tower blocks
- traffic congestion
- poor social, educational and recreational provision
- overcrowding

Economic problems
- unemployment
- lack of skilled workers
- poverty and low incomes
- poor access
- declining industry
- lack of space for new industry
- high land values

Social problems
- crime problems
- falling birth rates
- concentrations of very old and young
- endemic illness
- lots of single parents
- political activism
- high concentrations of ethnic groups
- dysfunctional families

- There is still too little being done to overcome the problems that continue to plague inner city areas.
- However, several high profile projects have moved the debate on, e.g. *London's Docklands Project* and the *Cardiff Bay Development Project*

Managing cities

- As urbanisation progresses many problems have to be tackled.
- Without proper planning and management, problems can get out of hand.

LEDCs

- Governments and aid institutions have favoured big capital projects, though the real needs in the developing world city may be more subtle.
- LEDC's need an environment in which jobs are available and small businesses can flourish.
- There needs to be recognition of land rights.
- Public transport and housing needs to be provided at reasonable cost.
- The provision of child care, schooling, and health services is a must.
- There has to be fair application of law and order.

MEDCs

- Concerns focus on overcrowding, loss of agricultural land, urban sprawl and congestion, dereliction of inner cities and pollution.
- This has spawned a raft of uniquely 'western' solutions.

The green belt

- This is land that is protected from industrial, transport and housing development and reserved for farming, forestry and wildlife areas.
- There is a clear and obvious benefit from having and retaining green belt land, but pressures for development, especially in the SE will test governmental resolve to the full.

New towns

- The 1946 New Towns Act was put in place to provide homes for overspill populations from the biggest of the UK's inner cities.
- They were to attract and develop new industrial agglomerations.
- They were meant to be self-contained communities separate from the cities.
- Most are near London, though successive legislation has distributed them over the whole of the UK.

Examiner's Tip

Inner-city problems constitute an appropriate theme for frequent inclusion at AS Level.

Progress check

1 Why do the inner cities of MEDCs continue to house the biggest proportion of urban poor?

2 Why are there often few cheap houses to be found in rural locations?

3 (a) What is the rural-urban fringe?

   (b) There is competition and conflict for land in this area. Outline some of the problems that have to be dealt with in the rural urban fringe.

4 'Some rural areas in the UK are backward compared to more urbanised areas.' Why might this be so?

5 'World-wide urbanisation is here to stay.' What trends are exhibited by current urbanisation?

6 (a) Why are many inner-city areas in need of renewal and renovation?

   (b) Many inner-city areas have been hugely improved and re-urbanisation has occurred. What are the economic, social and political causes of this process?

7 What is spontaneous settlement?

8 On a basic outline of a city or town you know well, draw on the functional zones, transport features, new morphological additions, open space, etc.

Answers on page 92–93

Industry

Classification

- If you asked anyone 50 years ago what the word 'industry' meant they might have replied 'mining and manufacturing'.
- Ask that same group of people today and their response would be vastly different.
- It is now one of many economic activities which include transport, communications, services, tourism and mining and manufacturing.
- **Industry is work performed for an economic gain.**
- To make the study of economic activity a little easier a traditional classification or grouping of activities is often used and referred to, as below:

Primary activity

- Involves extraction or collection or the early processing of resources from activities such as quarrying, mining, forestry and farming.
- The activity is resource based and is the basis for secondary industry.

Secondary activity

- Manufacturing, processing and assembly are the main activities; they change or transform the products of primary activity.
- The value of the raw material is increased by secondary activity, and locations do vary.
- *Heavy industry* adds bulk.
- *Light industry* is smaller scale, making TVs, etc.

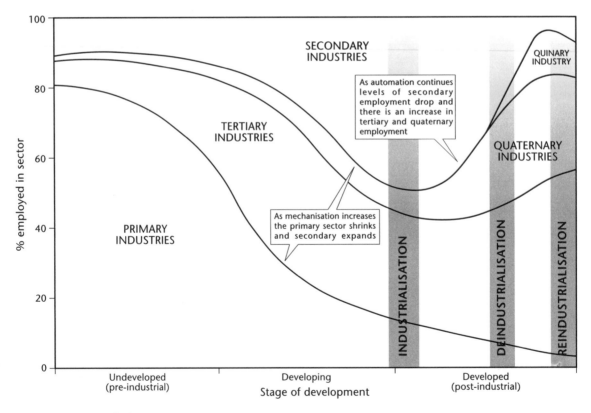

Tertiary activity

- Provides a service to customers, thus it is market oriented.
- This area of work includes transport, shopping, teaching, office, banks, doctors, etc.

Quaternary activity

- The main service provided is information and expertise.
- With the advent of computers, internet and fax these industries are mobile and can locate just about anywhere.
- Many locate in universities or research and development centres.
- Marketing, advertising and research and development are themselves quaternary activities.

Quinary activity

- Includes education, Government, health and research.
- *Fourastie's Model* (summarised opposite), relates the approximate sizes of sectors today, based on their levels of economic development.
- It also indicates the approximate time frame of **industrialisation**, **de-industrialisation** and **re-industrialisation**.

European trends

- Secondary or manufacturing industry formed the cornerstone for most MEDC economies, leading countries through phases of economic development and increasing prosperity.
- However, the requirements of industry are changing.
- No longer do they need to be located at, or near, their raw material.
- They need locations that are spacious and accessible with a rich labour market.
- *'Regional' industrial centres* (e.g. the Ruhr, Germany and the West Midlands, UK), Inner City and CBD sites are in decline.
- *Greenfield sites* and *city periphery sites* are popular now.
- This fundamental change in location will continue apace as de-industrialisation is completed and rationalisation, restructuring, globalisation and re-industrialisation gathers pace!

The new industrial core

- Manufacturing has undoubtedly declined in Europe – the service sector is now the largest employer and revenue producer.
- A variety of measures can be used to establish the new European core.
- The highest GDPs are found from SE England through the Netherlands, Belgium and the western part of Germany.
- The poorest areas are the peripheral areas of Spain, Ireland, Portugal, Southern Italy and Greece.
- Unemployment shows a similar pattern to GDP.
- *'Hot banana'* is the term coined for the core area of Europe; based on the curved shape of the countries involved.
- The area covers only 11% of Europe, but accounts for over 40% of output.
- Other key factors include the effective and efficient transport network contained in this area, the skill of the labour force and the system of tax and financial assistance the area accepts.
- The biggest growth regions are the Paris, London and Amsterdam triangle; the Ruhr basin; various islands of innovation (e.g. Toulouse); and those areas that have attracted finance (i.e. Valencia, Ireland and Scotland).

Examiner's Tip

Remember many traditional city industries have 'suburbanised' with the urban populations.

De-industrialisation

- Generally relates to the decline in jobs in the manufacturing sector of the employment structure.
- There are usually valid causes, but it can be due to inefficient production methods and inadequate infrastructure.
- *Reasons* include:
  - decline in the smokestack industries
  - depletion of raw materials
  - the cost of raw materials
  - new technology and automation
  - rationalisation
  - a lack, or removal of subsidies
  - the rise of the service sector in terms of employment
  - competition from cheaper imports
  - diversification and mergers of larger companies
  - mismatch between manufactured exports and imports
  - effect of over-zealous trade unions
- *Characteristics* include:
  - coincident with periods of economic depression
  - sudden onset and massive scale disrupting local balance of payments
  - concentrated in the 19th-century industrial cities of Europe and the USA
  - makes redundant millions of manufacturing workers
  - leaves behind much more competitive manufacturing industry.

Globalisation

The rise of the NICs

- During the 1980s manufacturing began to shift globally to the NICs (**Newly Industrialised Countries**).
- In the 1990s these have been challenged by the RICs (**Rapidly Industrialising Countries**) of Asia and Latin America. This was due to a combination of de-industrialisation in the MEDCs and the successful combination of factors associated with the outstanding growth of the NICs.

Causes of success in the NICs

- Single most important force is the growth of the TNC (**TransNational Corporations**). They bring:

  - huge inflows of capital
  - new technology
  - above average wages
  - greater employment opportunities
  - more industry to a region (see Myrdal p. 85)
  - increased trade.

- *Command capitalism* – Government help and encouragement.
- A ready supply of *cheap industrial labour* from rural to urban drift, *resulting from greater agricultural productivity or decline.*
- *Foreign capital*, not just from TNC growth, is attracted to NICs.
- *Ready markets*: appropriate industries were introduced to capitalise upon a consumer boom in the MEDCs at a time when MEDC industry was in decline (e.g. toys, garments, shoes, leather and plastics).
- *Capital* amassed from their huge growth available for reinvestment.
- Shifting production from low quality, low order goods to the more sophisticated, i.e. microchips (e.g. Samsung, Goldstar, Daewoo).
- Establishing their own TNCs in MEDCs e.g. Daewoo and Hyundai.

Examiner's Tip

Rather than traditional economic geography, AS will undoubtedly focus on globalisation, considerations of the legacy of former production methods, and the impacts of industrial activity on the environment.

Problems associated with rapid industrial growth

Environmental
- High emissions of a range of pollutants, e.g. CO_2, bacterial and heavy metals.
- Deforestation.

Economic
- The growth of industry has left the infrastructure behind, i.e. intermittent electricity supply and poor road and distribution networks internally in many NICs.
- Manufacturing drains newly won cash, there is a move, therefore, away from costly heavy industry.
- TNCs take vast profits out of the host country.

Human
- Workers are exploited: immigrant and child labour is common and maintains many 'economies'.
- Western 'values' are abhorred in many of the Muslim NICs.

Positive spin-offs from NIC's growth
- Foreign currency has allowed education, health, infrastructure, public health (sanitation, etc.) to be provided for and managed properly.
- The number below the poverty line has fallen.
- Industry has developed: increasingly international markets are exploited and developed; not for low-order cheap goods, but for high technology /state of the art products.

The future
- Asian NICs are likely to try to enter Chinese markets.
- NICs will increasingly widen their industrial base beyond that originally set up; loosen ties with MEDCs and their financial investment.
- Beware ... the bubble bursting, e.g. South Korea's economic collapse in 1997, the run on the Yen in 1998 and 1999, and the knock-on effect on imports from Australia and the USA. Growth based on high borrowing will be avoided in the future!
- Import control (i.e. GATT/WTO) is likely to impact on the MEDCs.

The importance of high technology: the new global industry
- Much of today's industry and economic activity is global in nature; or is multi-continental, with a range of activities taking place in many countries.
- The predominant feature of high-tech industry is its globalisation in the last 25 years.
- This vital industry has massive effects and implications for the MEDCs of the world.
- Its effect on our way of life is without question and its contribution to our wealth is paramount.
- High-tech industries (e.g. ICT, telecommunications, consumer electronics, computer software, pharmaceuticals, etc.) all demand an innovative and committed workforce.
- The manufactured product is sophisticated and contains, or is the result of, the latest technology.
- Globalisation is brought about by the TNCs who search the globe for the cheapest labour, the largest markets and lowest costs.
- Very roughly one would expect microelectronics to dominate in the USA, Europe and Japan, and consumer production to dominate in the Asian NICs.

Examiner's Tip

Much of the recent 'industrialisation' in the world has occurred in LEDCs. At AS Level comparisons will always be sought with other less successful developing world countries.

Re-industrialisation or tertiarisation

- The key area of industrial growth linked to re-industrialisation is tertiarisation – the growth of the service sector.
- Service industries employ upward of 18 million in the UK alone.
- The industry affects every part of the economy and de-industrialised economy, changing and adapting as different phases of the industrial process develop.
- In the UK there is a high degree of inequality in levels of service activity across the UK, because of:
  - London's dominance
  - the pre-dominance of the SE
  - decentralisation.
- Tertiarised activity can be classified into consumer and producer services.

Consumer services, those which deal with the general public

- Patterns of consumer provision have to match population distribution, e.g. rural West Norfolk has less people and fewer services in comparison with the Norwich area.

Locational factors

- *Accessibility*, in terms of transport, but also high quality telephonic links, fax and web connections: ICT is crucial.
- *Labour force*: close and plentiful. Service industries are major employers; many offer services 24 hours a day 365 days a year!
- *Land prices*: huge capital start-up costs mean that cheaper out-of-town locations are preferred.
- Being footloose ensures that consumer services can be fairly flexible in terms of their approach to location and potential market.
- On the whole, consumer services still tend to 'hug' centres of population.

Producer services, provide for other services

- We are concerned here with management, public relations, computer services, etc.
- Much of the business is face to face, or by phone, fax or video-conferencing.
- As expected, producer services locate near their customers' industries.

Characteristics

- Low capital start-up.
- Labour intensive, with the product being wholly dependent upon the standards applied by the staff and workers.
- Most jobs tend to be white-collared (i.e. non-manual).
- In a sense the user or purchaser of the service is part of the production process.

- SE England has seen a massive growth in this sector being close to the capital's decision makers and the research centres at the eastern end of the Thames Valley.

Examiner's Tip

Be able to explain reasons for increased tertiary activity, i.e. increased demand, improvements in technology, demographic change, de-industrialisation and tertiarisation.

Economic and industrial location models

Myrdal's cumulative causation

- A systems diagram explaining the process that increases inequalities between regions.
- Traditionally referred to manufacturing industry but has been adapted to model the new siting of service industry in the urban periphery.
- The initial advantages of the new periphery site are likely to be strong infrastructural links, strong social acceptance of change, moves lead by entrepreneurs. The expanding service industry attracts employment and other linked employment, and wealth begins to grow.
- Multiplier effects encourage agglomeration and the site becomes increasingly favoured and successful.
- In the traditional industrial centre, the city centre, backwash causes a downward economic spiral. This state is not permanent though, as spread effects quickly reduce the imbalance initially created and the core sees some redevelopment.

Merits

- The model has many merits, it does work best at a national or international level, but can be successfully applied at local levels too.
- It seeks to explain the growth of industry as a series of linked relationships, on an undefined timescale.

Rostows model of economic growth

- Attempts to explain the development of economies in five linear stages or sequences.
- Rostow's graph plots time against expanding wealth.

Merits

- a useful starting point for understanding development.
- It can be used in conjunction with cumulative causation.

Limitations

- It is analogy based.
- It is based on Europe, USA and Japan.
- Growth in economies can occur without development.

The product cycle

- Based on work by R. Vernon, this cycle is used to study industrial location and regional development.

Merits

- *It is simple.*
- Everyday objects can be exemplified.

Limitations

- Assumes the product is created in its final form and that it doesn't evolve.
- Improvements to a product are ignored.

Examiner's Tip

Models and theories to do with economic development are frequently evolutionary in nature. As most LEDCs have only recently industrialised, comparison questions, with MEDCs, make frequent appearances at AS Level.

(Continued next page)

Economic and industrial location models

Classic theories

- A variety of explanations and themes have been put forward in an attempt to explain industrial location.
- Chronologically they are:

Alfred Weber (1909)

- Saw manufacturing as a series of least-cost locations or points.
- He considered the weight of raw materials, the weight loss or gain during manufacturing and transport costs.
- It was therefore a raw material/market oriented theory.
- He recognised the importance of agglomerations.

Harold Hotelling (1929)

- Saw the manufacturing process as sites that would provide the largest revenue return.
- He recognised there would be competition, decision-making and that producers locate at a market centre.

August Losch (1957)

- The emphasis here was on demand and that with distance demand would drop with increasing transport costs.

These three theories were based on assumptions about the physical landscape, transport costs and that man was a rational decision-maker!

Allan Pred (1967)

- Worked not with locational decision-making but with an emphasis on behaviour.
- He recognised that businesses vary in the information that is available, how to use it and the importance of non-economic decisions.
- The size of companies is also important in Pred's theory. His conclusion was that man looks for a variety of micro-, meso- and macro-scale conditions before deciding on an industrial location.

David Smith (1971)

- Smith's model defines the area where total revenue exceeds total costs.
- Industry will locate within the area in which profit can be made and not beyond this area where losses are made.

Current theories:

'Smokestack is replaced by Sunrise Industry'.

Doreen Massey (1989)

- Layers of investment theory, where the idea of inertia and missed labour opportunities are important to eventual location, i.e. the use of female labour.

Dunford (1989)

- Sunrise industry locations are flexible in terms of material used, production, labour and transport costs.

Castree (1992)

- Suggests that the footloose nature of industry means Weber's ideas are now redundant, with the exception of agglomeration.

Examiner's Tip

Be aware that industrial location has been studied for some 100 years and continues to be investigated, it will always loom large at AS Level.

Primary and secondary industry in the UK

Coal mining

- Industrial development in the UK was based on coal.
- Over time the industry has been threatened by oil and by aggressive European competition.
- As the European coal industry grew, our own collapsed wrecking lives and economies.

One hundred years of mining

- *1900* Continued expansion and the peak of coal production to a growing and energy-hungry heavy industry.
- *Since 1945* Residential and industrial use has collapsed. Replaced by power stations. Improvements in technology and mechanisation have closed high-cost, low-production pits.
- *Since 1960* Cheap oil purchases from the Middle East reduced demand further.
- *1973* Energy crises ensured the Government's determination to develop other cheaper sources of power.
- *1974* Last ditch attempt to 'rescue coal', with flagship projects at Selby and the Vale of Belvoir.
- *Early 1980s* Imports flood onto the UK market from Europe and further afield.
- *1984 to 1985* Miners strike, the death knell for coal.
- *1990s* Concern for the environment leads to a reassessment of coal's future use in the UK.
- *1992 to 1993* 31 pits closed, 30 000 lost their jobs.
- *1994* 18 000 miners employed. When the industry was nationalised in 1947 there were 750 000 miners!

The car industry

- The private car is big business in terms of employment and sales in the UK.
- However, our car-based economy is threatened by:
  - changes in traditional production costs and markets
  - environmental costs such as recycling, pollution and the use of land for parking and roads.
- The market for cars grew steadily in the early 1980s.
- After 1988 the British Motor Industry changed rapidly with up to 50 000 job losses and nearly a one million drop in car sales despite increased productivity.
- Recession and our departure from the ERM can account for the bulk of these changes.
- In 1993 Ford announced losses of £1 000 000/day and with recession biting hard in Europe UK car sales to the continent all but stopped.
- Faced with increased costs and resulting redundancies the industry had to make changes.
- *Mergers* occurred: Rover with BMW; VW, Audi with Seat and Skoda.
- These make possible massive economies of scale, and make the companies extremely competitive.
- *Just in time production* (JIT).
  - This system, devised by the Japanese, has had a remarkable effect on car production, reducing costs and overheads.

Examiner's Tip

Although it isn't widely examined a knowledge of what's gone before is vital, if one is to understand what's going on now within industry.

(Continued next page)

Primary and secondary industry in the UK

- Computer links are used to globalise factory production plans, specific sales data and delivery systems, minimising the need for surplus stocks at the factories and, thereby, releasing capital for other purposes.
- Nissan UK estimate they have cut 2.4 million miles off the delivery mileage for the Micra through this system, with savings being passed on to the motorist.
- The British car industry looks set for a future in research and development rather than manufacturing. (In March 2000 Ford announced the closure of their Dagenham Fiesta plant.)

Examiner's Tip

Case study material is crucial in many AS Level industrial questions. The 'unique' nature of the manufacturing industry and rigour of globalised economic activity make it ideal 'periodical' material. Collect, save and use as much information from newspapers and magazines as possible.

Progess check

1 (a) Why has industry become increasingly less important in the MEDCs?

   (b) Describe the effects of manufacturing decline on any named area in the UK.

   (c) In LEDCs employment in manufacturing industry is relatively low; why is this?

2 Why do multi-national motor firms locate different parts of their operations in different parts of the world?

3 (a) Account for changes in tertiary activity over the last 30 years.

   (b) Using the diagram in the settlement section of this book (page 77) account for the changes in location of retail activity.

4 Construct a flow diagram/mind map to show the range of factors that affect the location of industry. Base it on the chronology offered in this section.

5 Why has industrial growth in LEDCs concentrated in the SE Asian area?

6 What are the causes, evidence and impact of de-industrialisation?

7 How do governments influence patterns of industrial location and growth?

8 Past and present manufacturing activity has had a dramatic effect on the environment. Outline some of these effects.

Answers on page 93–94

Progress check answers

Shaping the Earth

1 Each heading needs to be developed:
   (a) Jigsaw fit – continents must therefore have been closer once upon a time.
   (b) Earthquake distribution – along plate boundaries. They result from movements along the boundary.
   (c) Palaeomagnetism – describes how iron particles in lava have frozen in the direction of the earth's magnetic field at the time they cooled.

2 (a) The burden or weight forces down the continental land masses.
   (b) Land masses become buoyant and the continental levels recover.

3 (a) and (b) are straight forward.
   (c) slab pull/push and glide.

4 Plume diagram under a moving plate needs to be drawn.

5 • geothermal energy
   • tourism encouraged
   • new land
   • rich agricultural land
   • rare minerals
   • building materials

6 (a) P – waves fast / solid and liquid / compressional
      S – waves slow / solid / displacement and right-angled
      L – waves slow / solid / rolling
   (b) S, P and L waves

7 No answer here, it depends on the case study chosen.

8 Use diagrams similar to those in the text.

The atmosphere

1 Weather = day to day changes
   Climate = average weather experienced at a place at particular time of the year.

2 Imbalances in energy receipts between the equator and the poles set in motion the general circulation.

3 **Relative Humidity** = ratio of actual water vapour to the maximum that can be held expressed as a %.
   Environmental Lapse Rate = the vertical distribution of temperature, it averages 6.5°C/km.
   DALR = rate of cooling of a parcel of air. DALR is 10°C/km.
   SALR = rate of cooling of a saturated parcel of air. SALR is 7°C/km.
   Stability = cool air that is dense and heavy returning to its original level.
   Instability = air that is buoyant and less dense rising freely.

4 Well covered in the text. Rehearse your answer here.

5 Causes and consequences are well documented in the text.

6 Weather effects and human activity is covered thoroughly in the text.

7 This is where your knowledge of ozone comes into its own.

8 • Precipitation
   • Wind
   • Humidity and evaporation are all affected in various ways.

Soils and ecosystems

1 (a) See the text of this book.

(b) **Climate**
- high rainfall
- cold

Vegetation
- Acid vegetation – heathers and coniferous trees
- polyphenols encourage acidification. These naturally occurring alcohols are released as vegetation rots down.

(c) • liming
- manuring to return nitrogen and biotic debris
- deep ploughing – to break up the hard pan
- drainage.

2 **Temperate**
- high precipitation
- cold and wet
- vegetation breaks down relatively slowly
- annual loss of leaves

Tropical
- Precipitation > evaporation
- hot and wet
- vegetation breaks down rapidly
- low acidity
- continuous fall of leaves.

3 **Podsolisation** – is rapid leaching caused by precipitation > evaporation, eluviation occurs and cheluviation contributes too.

Leaching – removal of cation nutrients and clays in solution.

Calcification – moisture drawn up through the soil. Evaporation > precipitation.

Eluviation – washing of particles of soil from high to low areas of the profile.

4 (a) **Texture** – shake in a bottle – let it settle. Measure the depths of the layers.

Structure – involves rolling moist soil around in the hands and moulding different shapes.

Acidity – use indicator paper.

Organic content – involves weighing and burning.

(b) • leached near watershed
- thin soil on valley sides
- alluviated soil lower down the profile
- waterlogged soil at the valley floor
- thick soil near the slope foot.

5 Use the detail from the page spread 26–27

6 (a) Use the diagram on page 30

(b) Primary succession = occurs on bare ground /areas previously lacking vegetation.
Secondary succession = areas changed by fire, human activity, etc.

7 For both parts of this question there are clear points made in the text of the book.

Hydrology

1 (a) Basic hydrological diagram needs to be drawn, with transfers and processes added similar to the text.

(b) • degree of antecedent moisture
- vegetation cover
- soil type – texture and structure
- slope angle, etc.

2 The balance of erosion and deposition determines the grade of the river. This is affected by variations in sea level, and its rejuvenational effects.

3 Efficiency is based on variations in the hydraulic radius.

4 Hjulström's studies involved plotting stream velocity against particle size. High velocities move bigger particles, etc.

5 Valley features relate to mass movement and slope foot variations. There are obvious variations in scale. Valley features have a strong link to channel processes.

6 Basic conclusion is that water is delivered at a different rate, the rest is in the text! Flood hydrographs enable peaks of flow to be predicted and therefore determine when floods are likely to occur.

7 • spread of urbanisation
   • deforestation
   • agricultural activity causes increased run-off, into clogged eutrified streams.

Coasts

1 Because inland areas, i.e. rivers have even more obvious management than coastal areas. Also changes occur most rapidly on coasts.

2 The link has to be made between erosion based on the concentration of energy on headlands and the dissipation of energy into bays. The dynamic effect being to straighten the coastline.

3 (a) Energy is lost rapidly on steep beaches and erosion occurs. The opposite occurring on shallow beaches.

   (b) • longshore drift
       • shallowness of the sea
       • supply of sand

       They tend to form when there is a change in direction of the coastline, e.g. at river estuaries, coast directional changes.

4 For example, a stack. Erosional processes need to be fully eluded to as does wave height, strength and duration of wind and waves, geology/lithology, exposure etc. …

5 Most hard engineering is both expensive and detrimental to the coastline because of destructive downstream effects.

   Sustainable alternatives include: retention of dune systems, saltmarsh regeneration, replenishment, farmland allowed to flood, the formation of new mudflats, do-nothing scenarios.

6 Sea-level variations based on global warming, etc. is the likely concern here, based on the fact that so many live so close to the coastline.

Population

1 All words have been taken from the text; rehearse the answers by re-reading the relevant section.

2 (a) Population growth would outstrip supply.
   (b) Boserupian Theory 'necessity is the mother of invention'.

3 Answers are well documented in the text, rehearse them here.

4 Under- and over-population are more usual. Talk about carrying capacities, resources becoming more productive (i.e. Green Revolution), new resources being discovered, impact of migration and social change.

5 • increasing dependency ratios
   • burden on the workers
   • changes in homes needed
   • changing labour needs
   • value of the 'grey' pound
   • decreased/increased mobility

6 **Anti-natalist** – forced or voluntary reduction in population, e.g. China's one-child policy.

   Transmigration – Population moved to other unexploited parts of the country, e.g. in Indonesia.

   Immigration control – limits to numbers of people allowed to enter the country, e.g. Australia.

7 Depends on what countries are chosen, but explanations will be based on:

LEDCs
- wide base
- concave shape to sides
- dependency
- narrow tip
- high BR and DR

MEDCs
- falling birth rates
- high life-expectancy
- bulges and booms

8 **Usefulness**
- descriptive
- predictive
- stimulates R and D
- offers an insight into differences between MEDCs and LEDCs

Limitations
- Eurocentric
- no migration included
- no 5th stage
- reasons for change are different in LEDCs and MEDCs

Settlement

1 - cycle of deprivation
  - employment discrimination
  - failure of regeneration efforts.

2 - counter-urbanisation
  - second homes.

3 (a) The rural-urban fringe is the zone of transition between rural and urban areas. Typical land use:
  - agriculture
  - mining
  - industrial estates
  - airports
  - low-density housing
  - bypasses

  (b) Social conflict occurs because of:
  - the influx of urbanites
  - the need for lots of new housing
  - farmer/urban conflicts
  - decentralisation of industry into/onto greenfield sites on/in the rural urban continuum
  - environmental and ecological extremist groups
  - recreation.

4 - high unemployment
  - lower average incomes
  - declining local shops
  - shortage of low-rent housing
  - declining local services
  - lots of out-migration
  - little culture
  - youths not occupied

5 - majority of world population will be urbanised
  - MEDCs generally exhibit highest levels of urbanisation
  - LEDC cities have high densities of population
  - Numbers of LEDC cities are increasing
  - Largest cities will be in LEDCs come mid-century
  - Numbers of large cities are increasing
  - Rural LEDCs are on the way out!

6 (a) Because of:
  - poverty and unemployment
  - poor housing
  - derelict land
  - poor and inadequate roads
  - public transport is inadequate
  - poor facilities

(b) **Economic**
  - gentrified /converted and renovated houses make money
  - rent gap theory (high rents can be afforded).

  Social
  - young rich are drawn to culture and urban opportunities.

  Political
  - change in government /urban policy.

7
  - low cost housing, squatter or spontaneous settlements are built on land neither owned or rented by the inhabitants
  - there are few services
  - it is sited on marginal land (slopes /land liable to flooding)
  - houses are built from waste
  - homes are densely packed together
  - homes are built by the inhabitants.

8 Should include:
  - service activity – central and sub-urban
  - housing – range of centuries, styles and suburban and central housing
  - industry – derelict sites, industrial estates and science parks
  - railways, roads, parks and airports, etc…

Industry

1 (a)
  - cheaper to import
  - exhaustion of resources
  - decline of manufacturing
  - new cheaper replacements
  - problems of over-production.

(b)
  - less money for the council
  - collapse of linked industry
  - less money from taxes
  - wealth of area declines
  - decline in services
  - less demand for some services
  - loss of skilled workers
  - out-migration.

(c)
  - lack of crucial resources
  - over-exploitation of resources in the country
  - poor education
  - poorly developed markets
  - mechanisation.

2
  - low labour costs
  - weak environmental laws
  - proximity to markets
  - host-government incentives.

3 (a)
  - rationalisation
  - increased demand
  - improved technology
  - demographic changes
  - de-industrialisation.

(b) • congestion is less
   • high land prices are avoided
   • more space
   • accessible
   • purpose-built premises.

4 Ideas to do with:
   • ownership
   • site
   • environment
   • raw materials
   • energy
   • market
   • labour
   • capital
   • transport
   • government.

5 • trade opportunities provided by Japan
   • investment from Japan
   • high standard of education
   • low labour costs
   • political stability.

6 **Causes**
   • resources are all gone
   • importance of services
   • poor management
   • mechanisation
   • rationalisation
   • overseas competition
   • deglomeration.

   Evidence
   • recession = decline
   • manufacturing employment decreases
   • urban to rural shift in manufacturing.

   Impacts
   • social – unemployment
   • economic – leads to disinvestments
   • political – N v S divide, assisted status
   • last-minute attempts at diversification.

7 • assisted status assigned
   • support from EU and national government
   • enterprise status in some areas.

8 • air pollution
   • spillages into air/rivers
   • industrial landscapes
   • groundwater pollutes
   • subsidence in many areas.

Index